Nelson *Mathematics* 5

Workbook

Series Authors and Senior Consultants

Marian Small • Mary Lou Kestell

Workbook Authors

Carole Adam • Anne Cirillo

Kathy Kubota-Zarivnij • Rosita Tseng Tam

NELSON

NELSON

Nelson Mathematics 5
Workbook

Series Authors and Senior Consultants
Marian Small, Mary Lou Kestell

Authors
Carole Adam, Anne Cirillo, Kathy Kubota-Zarivnij, Rosita Tseng Tam

Reviewers
Grace Brereton, Peel District School Board,

Sharon Bowerman Rainbow District School Board

Director of Publishing
David Steele

Publisher, Mathematics
Beverley Buxton

Project Manager, K–8
David Spiegel

Senior Program Manager
Shirley Barrett

Workbook Program Manager
Alan Simpson

Developmental Editor
Nancy Andraos

Executive Managing Editor, Development & Testing
Cheryl Turner

Executive Managing Editor, Production
Nicola Balfour

Senior Production Editor
Gary Burford

Copy Editor
Riça Night

Editorial Assistant
Megan Robinson

Senior Production Coordinator
Sharon Latta Paterson

Production Coordinator
Franca Mandarino

Creative Director
Angela Cluer

Art Director
Ken Phipps

Art Management
ArtPlus Ltd., Suzanne Peden

Illustrators
ArtPlus Ltd.

Interior and Cover Design
Suzanne Peden

Cover Image
T. Kitchin/First Light

ArtPlus Ltd. Production Coordinator
Dana Lloyd

Composition
ArtPlus Ltd.

Library and Archives Canada Cataloguing in Publication

Nelson mathematics 5. Workbook / Marian Small ... [et al.].

ISBN 0-17-620098-3

1. Mathematics—Problems, exercises, etc.—Juvenile literature.

I. Small, Marian II. Title: Nelson mathematics five.

QA135.6.N485 2004 Suppl. 1
510   C2004-903005-1

Contents

Message to Parent/Guardian

This workbook has one page of practice questions for each lesson in your child's textbook *Nelson Mathematics 5*. The questions in the workbook are similar to the ones in the text, so they should look familiar to your child. The lesson Goal and the At-Home Help on each page will help you to provide support if your child needs it.

At the end of each chapter is a page of multiple-choice questions called "Test Yourself." This is an opportunity for you and your child to see how well she or he understands.

You can help your child explore and understand math ideas by making available some commonly found materials, such as

- string, scissors, and a ruler (for measurement)
- counters such as bread tags, toothpicks, buttons, or coins (for number operations and patterns)
- packages, cans, toothpicks, and modelling clay (for geometry)
- grid paper, magazines, and newspapers (for data management)
- board game spinners, dice, and card games (for probability)

You might also encourage your child to use technology if it is available, such as

- a calculator (for exploring number patterns and operations)
- a computer (for investigating the wealth of information that exists on the Internet to help people learn and enjoy math)

Visit the Nelson Web site at **www.mathk8.nelson.com** to view answers and find out more about the mathematics your child is learning.

It's amazing what you can learn when you look at math through your child's eyes! Here are some things you might watch for.

Checklist
☑ Can your child clearly explain her or his thinking?
☑ Does your child check to see whether an answer makes sense?
☑ Does your child persevere until the work is complete?
☑ Does your child connect new concepts to what has already been learned?
☑ Is your child proud of what's been accomplished so far?

1

2-D Patterns

Goal Use models and t-charts to record, extend, and make predictions about number patterns.

Look at design 1 of the capital letter F.
It has been made from 10 dots.

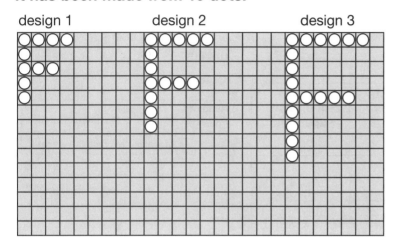

A **2-D pattern** has a length and a width.

For example, these shapes form a 2-D pattern.

□ ○ □ ○ □ ○

A **t-chart** has 2 columns. The data in both columns are related.

For example: As the number of songs increases by 1, the number of minutes of practice increases by 15 minutes.

Number of songs	Number of minutes of practice
1	10
2	25
3	40

1. How many dots are needed to complete design 4?

   _____

2. Predict the number of dots needed to complete design 5.

   _____

3. Draw design 4 and design 5.

4. Complete the t-chart to show the pattern.

Letter design	Number of dots
1	
2	
3	
4	
5	

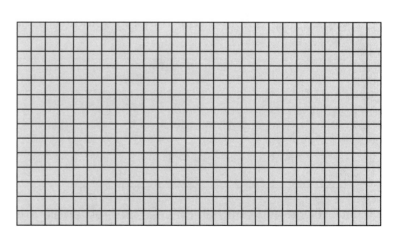

5. If you had a total of 50 dots, what design number would the letter F be?

   _____

2 Patterns in Tables

 Goal Create tables to display, predict, and extend patterns.

Apple crisp is a great recipe to make for many different sized groups. The recipe in the chart is complete for one class and partially complete for two classes.

Apple Crisp Recipe

Number of classes	Number of apples	Amount of butter (mL)	Amount of brown sugar (mL)
1	24	150	200
2	48	300	
3	72		
4			
5			

At-Home Help

A **table** usually has two or more columns of data. Each column has its own heading and is related to the other columns.

For example:

Number of times I make the recipe	Number of cups of water	Number of scoops of crystals	Number of people served
1	5	3	4
2			

1. Complete the recipe for all of the classes in the chart.

2. What pattern rules did you use to complete the table?

   _____

   _____

3. If you bought 200 apples, what is the greatest number of classes that could have apple crisp? Explain your thinking using numbers.

   _____

   _____

   _____

   _____

   _____

4. **a)** If one and one half classes wanted apple crisp, explain how you would calculate the amount of each ingredient.

   _____

   b) Calculate the amounts. Show your work.

Solve Problems Using Patterns

Goal   **Identify patterns to solve problems.**

1. What pattern could you use to add these numbers? Write a number sentence to show the pattern.

   $1 + 2 + 3 + 4 + \ldots + 37 + 38 + 39 + 40$

   _____

   _____

2. Use a pattern to add these numbers. Show your work.

   $15 + 25 + 35 + 45 + 55 + 65 + 75 + 85$

At–Home Help

Pairing numbers can help you find sums more easily. Try to find pairs that add up to the same number.

For example, to add

$1 + 3 + 5 + 7 + 9 + 11$

notice that $1 + 11$, $3 + 9$, and $5 + 7$ all add up to 12.

$$sum = (1 + 11) + (3 + 9) + (5 + 7)$$
$$= 12 + 12 + 12$$
$$= 36$$

---

3. Glynis is stacking boxes of candles for a store display.

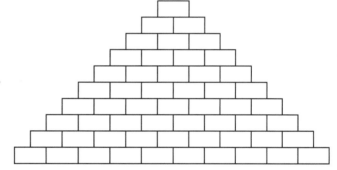

a) Make a plan that uses a pattern to find the number of boxes in the stack. Use number sentences and words.

   _____

   _____

b) Use your plan to find the total number of boxes in the stack.

c) How many boxes would there be in a stack that has 16 boxes in the bottom row? Explain your answer using number sentences and words.

   _____

   _____

   _____

4

3-D Patterns

 Goal Create a 3-D pattern and make predictions about its growth.

You will need linking cubes.

Look at the stack of boxes in Lesson 3 Question 3.

1. Make the first three stacks in the table using linking cubes. Determine how each stack is made from the one before. Then complete the table to show how many layers of boxes there will be if there are 210 boxes in total.

Number of layers	Number of new boxes	Total number of boxes
1	1	1
2	2	2 + 1 = 3
3	3	3 + 3 = 6
4		

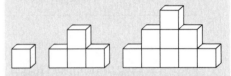

At–Home Help

A **3-D pattern** has a length, a width, and a height.

For example, these cubes form a 3-D pattern.

Organizing numbers in a table helps you see patterns.

For example:

Number of layers	Number of new boxes	Total number of boxes
1	1	1
2	3	3 + 1 = 4
3	5	5 + 4 = 9
4	7	7 + 9 = 16

total number of boxes
= number of new boxes
+ total number of boxes
in the line above

2. Explain what pattern you used to calculate your answer.

_____

_____

Number Patterns in Spreadsheets

 Goal **Create and identify patterns in spreadsheets.**

Yoshi is starting a new spreadsheet for a school sale of used equipment that includes small beanbags, medium hula hoops, and large basketballs.

	A	B	C	D
1	Sports equipment sale prices			
2	Number of items	Small	Medium	Large
3	1	$1.20	$2.40	$4.40
4	2	$2.40	$4.80	$8.80
5	3	$3.60	$7.20	$13.20
6	4	$4.80	$9.60	$17.60
7	5			
8	6			
9	7			
10	8			

At-Home Help

Spreadsheets are columns of data that are related. Each number in a spreadsheet has its own cell. To extend the numbers in a column, use one or more operations.

For example:
cost of 3 red shirts in cell
B5 = B3 + B4, or B5 = B3 × A5
total cost in cell D3 = B3 + C3

	A	B	C	D
1	Shirt prices			
2	Number of shirts	Red	Green	Total cost
3	1	$10.00	$15.00	$25.00
4	2	$20.00	$30.00	$50.00
5	3	$30.00	$45.00	$75.00

1. Complete the spreadsheet.

2. Write a pattern rule for column B by looking at the numbers in that column. Then write a pattern rule for columns C and D.

_____

_____

_____

3. Calculate the total cost. Show your work.

a) 6 small items and total cost

b) 3 small items, 2 medium items, and 7 large items and total cost

c) 10 items of each size and total cost

4. How can you get the answer in cell C5 from other cells?

Test Yourself

Circle the correct answer.

Use the table to answer Questions 1 and 2.

Number of teams	Number of players
1	4
2	8
3	16
4	32
5	64

1. What is the pattern in the second column of the table?

   A. The numbers increase by 4.

   B. The numbers double.

   C. The numbers increase by 3.

   D. The numbers increase by 2.

2. How many players would there be if there were 7 teams?

   A. 256   **B.** 212   **C.** 128   **D.** 246

3. Which table shows column 1 increasing by multiplying by 3 and column 2 doubling?

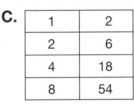

   A.

1	8
3	10
9	12
12	14

   B.

1	4
3	8
6	16
12	32

   C.

1	2
2	6
4	18
8	54

   D.

1	1
3	2
9	4
27	8

4. What are the next 2 numbers in this pattern?

   29, 30, 32, 35, 39, 44, _____, _____

   A. 50 and 55   **B.** 49 and 55   **C.** 50 and 57   **D.** 49 and 57

Test Yourself Page 2

5. Soccer teams go through a lot of equipment in one season. What numbers would complete the last row of this table?

Number of teams	Number of soccer nets	Number of soccer balls
1	2	5
3	6	15
5	10	25
?	?	?

A. 7, 14, 30　　　　**B.** 7, 14, 35　　　　**C.** 6, 15, 30　　　　**D.** 7, 15, 35

6. What will be the number of Xs in design 4 and design 7?

design 1

X X X
X   X

design 2

X X X X
X   X
X   X

design 3

X X X X X
X   X
X   X
X   X

A. 19 and 13　　　　**B.** 23 and 14　　　　**C.** 14 and 23　　　　**D.** 13 and 19

Use this spreadsheet to answer Questions 7 and 8.

	A	B	C	D
1	Cost of Cans			
2	Number of Cans	Small	Medium	Large
3	1	$0.50	$2.00	$3.25
4	2	$1.00	$4.00	$6.50
5	3	$1.50	$6.00	$9.75

7. What would be the total cost of 4 cans of each size?

A. $22.50　　　　**B.** $24.00　　　　**C.** $23.50　　　　**D.** $23.00

8. What is the pattern rule for column C?

A. Start at $2.00 and add $0.50 to each number going down column C.

B. Start at $2.00 and add $2.00 to each number going down column C.

C. Start at $2.00 and add $3.25 to each number going down column C.

D. Start at $2.00 and add $1.00 to each number going down column C.

1 Estimating 50 Thousand

Goal **Use numbers you know to estimate 50 thousand objects.**

1. Make a list of items in your home that you can count to 100.

   _____

   _____

   _____

2. Choose one item from your list. Count 2 sets of 100 and put them in a pile.

3. How many of those piles would make a quantity of 1000 items? Show your work.

4. How many piles of 1000 would make a quantity of 50 thousand items? Show your work.

5. Estimate what 50 thousand of those items would look like. How would you describe it to a friend?

   _____

   _____

   _____

6. Use another way to estimate 50 thousand of the same item. Describe your method in detail.

   _____

   _____

7. Choose another item from your list. Estimate what 50 thousand of these items would look like.

   _____

   _____

> **At-Home Help**
>
> To estimate 50 thousand, use familiar objects in smaller quantities.
>
> For example: Use 100 pennies. Put them in a pile in a shoebox. About how many piles of 100 will fill the shoebox?
>
> This answer can be used to estimate the number of boxes needed for 10 thousand pennies.
>
> This new answer can be used to estimate the number of boxes needed for 50 thousand pennies.

2 Reading and Writing Numbers

Goal **Read, write, and model five-digit numbers.**

1. A file on your computer is 15 827 bytes long.

   a) Write this number in words.

   _____

   b) Write this number in expanded form.

   _____

   c) Draw a representation of 15 827 using base ten blocks.

Ten thousands	Thousands	Hundreds	Tens	Ones

At–Home Help

Numbers can be represented in different ways.

For example, sixteen thousand eight hundred fifty-four is

16 854 in **standard form**,

10 000 + 6000 + 800 + 50 + 4 in **expanded form**, and

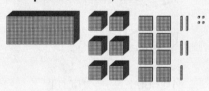

using base ten blocks

2. Write each number in words and in expanded form.

   a) 35 247 _____

   _____

   b) 40 409 _____

   _____

   c) 10 000 more than 50 030 _____

   _____

   d) 1000 less than 70 007 _____

   _____

3. Write each number in standard form.

   a) fifty thousand eleven _____ b) 50 000 + 8000 + 60 + 3 _____

4. Your class collected 21 347 pennies for a penny drive. Write 21 347 in words and in expanded form.

   _____

3 Renaming Numbers

Goal   **Rename numbers with up to five digits.**

Suppose an ice cream company created the largest milkshake ever made. The company made a milkshake that would fill 24 382 one-litre containers.

1. Find five different combinations of full containers that would hold this milkshake. Show your work and record your answers in the table below.

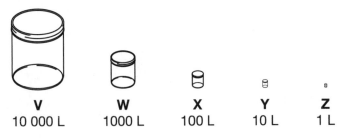

V	W	X	Y	Z
10 000 L	1000 L	100 L	10 L	1 L

Container V 10 000 L	Container W 1000 L	Container X 100 L	Container Y 10 L	Container Z 1 L
2	4	3	8	2

2. Draw 2 representations of 24 382 using base ten blocks.

Ten thousands	Thousands	Hundreds	Tens	Ones

CHAPTER 2

4

Comparing and Ordering Numbers

Goal Compare and order numbers with up to five digits.

1.

Blue Jays' opponents	Average attendance in Toronto	Average attendance at opponent's stadium
Orioles	20 572	27 955
Devil Rays	20 459	9048
Expos	31 571	12 782
Yankees	27 205	33 916
Angels	20 106	41 088

a) Which teams had a greater attendance when in their home stadium than in Toronto?

_____

b) Show the attendance of three games on the number line.

At-Home Help

When comparing and ordering numbers up to five digits, compare the digits in this order:
• ten thousand
• thousand
• hundred
• ten
• one

You can also compare and order numbers by their positions on a number line.

Inequality signs < and > show that one number is greater than another.

For example, 8 > 5 is read "eight is greater than five."

5 < 8 is read "five is less than eight."

2. Complete each number sentence using < or >.

a) 20 899 _____ 20 100   **c)** 45 072 _____ 47 072   **e)** 90 000 _____ 89 999

b) 3687 _____ 3675   **d)** 24 531 _____ 23 154   **f)** 19 560 _____ 20 650

3. Order each group of numbers from greatest to least using inequality signs.

a) 14 532   8927   41 536   50 001

_____

b) 67 013   6713   67 130   67 103

_____

4. Adrian collected pennies for a penny drive. He wrote the digits for the total number of pennies on separate cards. Each card had a 1, 8, 3, 5, or 4. The cards got all mixed up. He knew that the number of pennies was between 20 000 and 45 000. List three possibilities for the number of pennies.

CHAPTER 2

5

Rounding Numbers

Goal **Round numbers to the nearest ten thousand, thousand, and hundred.**

A doughnut machine has a counter to record the number of doughnuts made in a day. Yesterday the count was 36 471.

1. Round the number of doughnuts to the nearest hundred. Explain your answer.

36 400
36 500

____

At-Home Help

Numbers can be **rounded** to the nearest hundred, thousand, and ten thousand.

For example, 85 354 rounded
- to the nearest hundred is 85 400
- to the nearest thousand is 85 000
- to the nearest ten thousand is 90 000

A number line helps with rounding.

2. Round the number of doughnuts to the nearest thousand. Explain your answer.

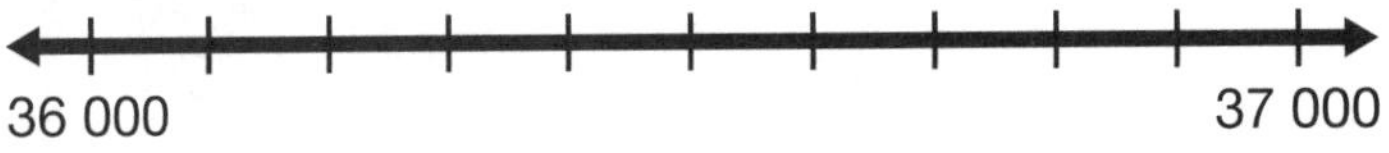
36 000
37 000

____

3. Use the number line to round the number of doughnuts to the nearest ten thousand. Explain your answer.

30 000
40 000

____

4. Round each number to the nearest hundred, thousand, and ten thousand.

a) 45 632 **b)** 60 119 **c)** 75 456

6 Communicate About Numbers in the Media

 Goal Evaluate the use of numbers in the media.

Gen is doing a science project on Canada geese. She found this information on a Web page.

> The Canada goose is well known for its V-shaped migratory flight pattern and characteristic honk.
>
> There are 11 geographical species, some with populations well over a million, and some with barely over one thousand.
>
> In 1991 there were 63 581 Canada geese in the United Kingdom.
>
> The largest goose is the giant, with a wingspan of more than 2 m and a mass under 10 kg. The smallest is the so-called "cackling" goose, which has a mass of only 1–2 kg.
>
> Between 1983 and 2000, the size of the urban wintering flock in Wichita grew from 1623 birds to over 15 000!

1. What numbers on the Web page do you find confusing?

_____

_____

_____

_____

2. Are all the numbers described in the same way?

_____

3. Do you agree with how the numbers 1623 and 15 000 are represented?

_____

_____

4. Where would you like to see a range given?

_____

7 Decimal Hundredths

Goal **Read, write, and represent decimal hundredths.**

1. In gym class, students practised long jump in the sandpit. Paige recorded her friends' jumps in a chart.

Long jump distances	
Sean	1.27 m
Dan	0.96 m
Lisa	1.36 m

At-Home Help

The number 1.35 is read "one and thirty-five hundredths."

This number can be represented on a metre stick number line.

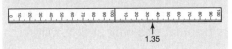

1.35

   a) Use words to represent each distance.

   _____

   _____

   _____

   _____

   b) Mark each distance on the metre stick number line.

2. Write each decimal number in standard form.

   a) six and seven hundredths _____

   b) five and ten hundredths _____

   c) fourteen and fifteen hundredths _____

   d) twenty-six hundredths _____

3. Write a decimal number in standard form to fit each description.

   a) 1 tenth greater than 4.16 _____

   b) 1 greater than 4.16 _____

   c) 1 hundredth greater than 4.16 _____

4. Sally's best long jump distance is 1.63 m. Write in words how you would read her distance.

   _____

8

Exploring Equivalent Decimals

Goal **Rename a decimal tenth as a decimal hundredth.**

1. Write a decimal tenth to describe the part of the grid that is shaded.

   _____

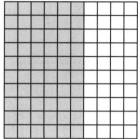

2. Write a decimal hundredth to describe the same part.

   _____

3. Shade in three more squares on the grid.

4. Write a decimal number for the total shaded part.

   _____

5. Write two ways to read this decimal number.

   _____

   _____

At-Home Help

Some decimal numbers can be read as tenths or hundredths.

For example, 0.30 can be read as
• "three tenths zero hundredths" or
• "thirty hundredths"

0.30 can be represented by the shaded part on this decimal grid.

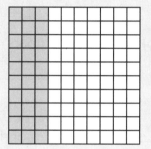

6. Show each decimal number on a grid by shading the appropriate squares.

   a) 0.70

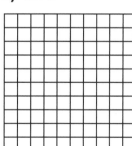

   b) 0.34

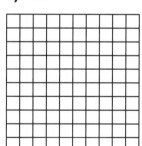

   c) 0.07

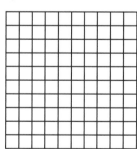

7. Which of these decimal hundredths can be expressed as decimal tenths? Give reasons for your choice.

   0.70   0.07   0.77   0.17

   _____

   _____

CHAPTER 2

Rounding Decimals

Goal Interpret rounded decimals, and round decimals to the nearest whole and to the nearest tenth.

1. Sarah rounded the length of her room to the nearest tenth of a metre. The length is 3.5 m.

3.4   3.5   3.6

a) Write the numbers that round up from 3.4 to 3.5.

_____

_____

b) Write the numbers that round down to 3.5.

_____

_____

At-Home Help

Decimal numbers can be rounded to the nearest whole number and the nearest tenth.

For example,
• 2.76 rounds up to 2.8
• 2.83 rounds down to 2.8

A number line helps with rounding.

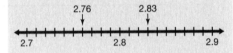

2.76   2.83

2.7   2.8   2.9

Both 2.76 and 2.83 round up to 3.

2. Lori needs 4.47 m of ribbon for a school play.

a) How much ribbon should she buy if ribbon is sold in lengths of whole metres?

_____

b) How much ribbon should she buy if ribbon is sold in lengths of tenths of a metre?

_____

3. Round each number to the nearest whole number and the nearest tenth.

a) 3.65   **b)** 7.03   **c)** 0.79   **d)** 7.93

_____   _____   _____   _____

_____   _____   _____   _____

4. A gardener needs 8.74 m of hose to water a lawn.

a) Round that length to the nearest tenth of a metre. _____

b) Should he buy a hose of that length or a different length? Explain.

_____

5. A number rounded to the nearest tenth is 7.9. What might the number be? List three possibilities.

_____

Comparing and Ordering Decimals

Goal **Compare and order numbers to decimal hundredths.**

1. Four members of the Sea Lions team competed in a relay race at a recent swim meet.

Swimmer	Stroke	Time
Zoe	Butterfly	2.54 s
Karilyn	Back	2.36 s
Andrea	Breast	2.75 s
Tanya	Freestyle	2.17 s

a) Who took the longest to swim her part of the race? What was her time?

_____

b) Who swam the fastest? What was her time?

_____

c) Order the times from shortest to longest.

_____

2. Draw a representation of Zoe's time using base ten blocks. Draw a hundreds block to represent 1.

Ones	Tenths	Hundredths

At-Home Help

When comparing and ordering decimal numbers to hundredths, represent the numbers using base ten blocks. Then compare the numbers.

For example:
6.84 can be represented as

Ones	Tenths	Hundredths

6.99 can be represented as

Ones	Tenths	Hundredths

Compare these two representations to pick the greater number.

3. Complete each number sentence using < or >.

a) 3.94 _____ 3.99   b) 46.03 _____ 47.06   c) 20.80 _____ 20.08

4. Order each group of numbers from least to greatest using inequality signs.

a) 0.23, 4.75, 6.35, 0.79, 4.57 _____

b) 5.15, 1.55, 0.51, 15.01 _____

c) 0.31, 0.13, 0.03, 0.01 _____

d) 6.1, 6.5, 6.06, 6.75, 6 _____

11 Counting Money

Goal Estimate, count, read, and write money amounts to $1000.

1.

a) Estimate the total. Explain your estimate.

_____

_____

b) Count the amount. Record it.

2. Describe or draw another set of coins and bills that make the same amount as in Question 1.

3. Describe or draw each amount using the fewest bills and coins possible.

   a) $16.54

   b) $281.34

4. Describe or draw $281.34 using more bills and coins.

Test Yourself

Circle the correct answer.

1. Which container would you choose to hold 50 thousand pennies?

   A. 5 shoeboxes   **B.** 5 lunchboxes   **C.** 5 bathtubs   **D.** 5 recycling boxes

2. Which representation is *not* the number 23 709?

   A. 20 000 + 3000 + 700 + 9

   B. 10 000 + 13 000 + 500 + 209

   C. 1 ten thousand + 13 thousand + 5 hundred + 20 tens + 9

   D. 10 000 less than 25 709

3. Which number sentence is incorrect?

   A. 20 899 < 28 100   **B.** 5697 > 5675

   C. 54 072 > 45 072   **D.** 34 521 < 34 125

4. Which number is rounded to the nearest hundred?

   A. 45 630   **B.** 75 000   **C.** 61 300   **D.** 10 001

5. What would 89 605 rounded to the nearest thousand be?

   A. 89 000   **B.** 89 600   **C.** 90 000   **D.** 90 600

6. Which number on the metre stick number line does the arrow point to?

   A. 1.60   **B.** 1.50   **C.** 1.57   **D.** 1.55

7. Which description fits for the number 2.67?

   A. two and six tenths   **B.** twenty-six and seven hundredths

   C. two hundred sixty-seven   **D.** two and sixty-seven hundredths

8. Which number is 1 tenth greater than 2.67?

   A. 3.78   **B.** 2.78   **C.** 3.67   **D.** 2.77

9. What would 7.86 rounded to the nearest tenth be?

   A. 8.0   **B.** 7.8   **C.** 8.6   **D.** 7.9

1 Evaluating Survey Results

Goal **Decide whether the results of a survey would likely apply to other groups of people.**

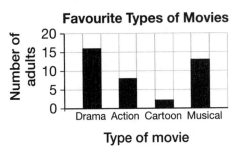

Favourite Types of Movies

At-Home Help

Biased results are results of a survey that apply to one group but are not likely to apply to another group.

1. Which type of movie was the favourite for the adults surveyed? Explain why adults would prefer these movies.

   _____

   _____

2. Explain why you think the overall results are accurate for this group of people.

   _____

   _____

   _____

3. Would the results of this survey likely apply to students in a Grade 1 class? Explain.

   _____

   _____

4. Predict the results if your class were surveyed. Create a graph of your prediction.

2 Broken-Line Graphs

Goal Make and use a broken-line graph to identify trends.

1.

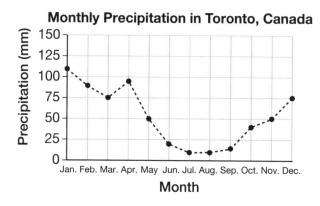

Monthly Precipitation in Toronto, Canada

At-Home Help

A **trend** in a graph refers to the general direction of data. The data can increase, decrease, or stay the same.

A **broken-line graph** is a graph in which data points are connected point by point.

What trends do you see in this broken-line graph?

_____

_____

_____

2. Make a broken-line graph of monthly precipitation in Sydney, Australia.

Monthly Precipitation in Sydney, Australia (mm)

Jan.	Feb.	Mar.	Apr.	May	Jun.	Jul.	Aug.	Sept.	Oct.	Nov.	Dec.
10	15	40	70	75	40	35	15	60	50	20	10

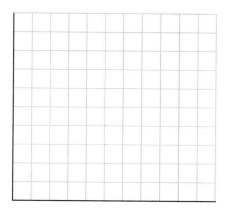

3. Compare your broken-line graph to the graph in Question 1. How are they similar?

3 Interpreting Circle Graphs

Goal Calculate the number represented by each part of a circle graph.

Thirty-two Grade 5 students answered a survey question about their favourite subject and most difficult subject. These circle graphs show the results.

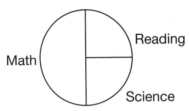

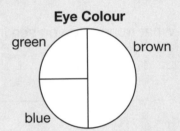

1. What fraction represents each part in the Favourite Subject graph?

   Math _____ Gym _____ Art _____

   Reading _____ Science _____

2. How many students are represented by each subject in the Favourite Subject graph?

   Math _____ Gym _____ Art _____

   Reading _____ Science _____

3. How many students are represented by each subject in the Most Difficult Subject graph?

   Math _____   Science _____   Reading _____

4. Suppose the survey applied to 40 students. How would your answers to Questions 2 and 3 change?

   _____

   _____

4

Bar Graphs with Intervals

 Goal **Use the range to estimate the size of intervals to construct a bar graph.**

Akiko recorded the number of metres jumped during a triple jump. She collected data from 24 students in her class.

Metres jumped (triple jump)

15	18	4	12	10	6
10	20	15	7	17	10
9	13	5	8	16	12
14	19	3	15	11	13

1. What is the range of the data?

_____

2. How many bars would you use if you made a bar graph of the data? Explain your choice based on the range. Include the intervals in your answer.

_____

_____

3. **a)** Make a tally chart for the data.

b) Draw a bar graph using your tally chart.

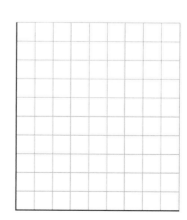

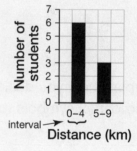

At-Home Help

Range is the spread of data. To find the range, look for the least and greatest data points.

For example, the range of the data is 53 to 80, which is 27 beats.

Heart Rates (beats in 1 min)

70	60	53
80	74	70
70	72	78

Before drawing some bar graphs, it is better to group data. **Intervals** refer to the size of the groups. All intervals should be the same size.

For example: Six students cycled between 0 and 4 km, and 3 students cycled between 5 and 9 km. The intervals on the graph are 0–4 and 5–9.

CHAPTER 3

Pictographs

Goal **Use whole and partial symbols to display data on a pictograph.**

Jose counted the number of birds on Memesagamesing Lake in Northern Ontario in July.

Type of bird	Number
Loon	75
Blue heron	40
Mallard duck	81
Cormorant	28

1. Draw a pictograph to show the data using whole and partial symbols. Make sure you show the scale.

2. Explain how you decided on the number of whole and partial symbols to show the number of birds.

_____

_____

3. Why are 81 and 28 difficult numbers to represent on the pictograph?

_____

_____

_____

4. What other scale could you use for the pictograph?

_____

At-Home Help

A **pictograph** is a graph that displays data using symbols. Each symbol represents a fixed number. Some data points can only be represented by using partial symbols.

For example, since 1 symbol represents 10 pies, 15 pies is represented with $1\frac{1}{2}$ symbols.

Types of Pies

Apple

Blueberry

Banana cream

Lemon meringue

⬭ = 10 pies

A **scale** on a pictograph shows the number represented by each symbol.

The scale for the pictograph above says that 1 symbol represents 10 pies.

Changing the Appearance of a Graph

Goal **Explain how changing the scale of a graph can affect its appearance.**

Drake made a graph to show the results of a survey about favourite desserts.

Favourite Desserts

Dessert	Number of people
Pie	150
Cake	127
Ice cream	106
Fruit cup	95

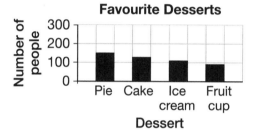

1. How does the scale affect the appearance of this graph?

_____

_____

2. Make another bar graph with a different scale to make the difference between the bars appear more dramatic.

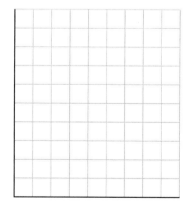

At-Home Help

The **scale** of a bar or line graph refers to the divisions on both the vertical and horizontal axes.

The scale of a graph can affect the appearance of data.

For example: The scale on the first graph goes from 0 to 200. This makes the difference between the bars not very clear.

The scale on the second graph goes from 0 to 20. The difference between the bars is very clear.

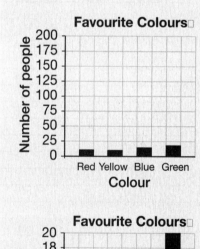

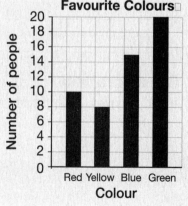

7 Graphing with Technology

 Goal Use graphing software to organize and display data.

Anton collected different types of materials for recycling. He was paid for each item he collected.

- 12 tins at 2¢ per tin
- 18 plastic containers at 5¢ per container
- 7 cardboard boxes at 10¢ per box
- 9 glass bottles at 15¢ per bottle

At-Home Help

A **spreadsheet** has columns and rows to organize data. Spreadsheets usually have columns of numbers that represent the result of math calculations.

1. Organize the data using a table or spreadsheet.

2. Construct a graph of your choice that would represent the data well. Use paper and pencil or a spreadsheet.

Mean and Mode

Goal Calculate the mean and identify the mode of a set of data.

You will need counters.

1. What is the mode of this group of numbers? Explain.

   6, 7, 4, 4, 9, 3, 2, 3, 7, 4, 9

   _____

2. **a)** What is the mean of 6, 7, and 8?

   _____

   b) What is the mean of 12, 14, and 16?

   _____

   c) What do you notice about the mean of each
   group of numbers in Parts **a)** and **b)**?

   _____

   _____

At-Home Help

Mean is the rearrangement of numbers to make equal shares.

For example, the mean of

0, 5, 1, 1, 3 is 2.

0 5 1 1 3

2 2 2 2 2

Mode is the number that occurs most often in a group of numbers.

For example, the mode of

0, 5, 1, 1, 3 is 1.

3. Calculate the mean and identify the mode of 32, 38, 33, and 33.

4. Create a group of four numbers that has a mode of 4 and a mean of 5.

   _____

Communicate About Graphs

Goal Evaluate the accuracy of a graph and suggest ways to present data accurately.

Leo recorded the cross-country running times of each student in his class. He then drew a bar graph.

Time (min)

4	8	4	12	10	6
13	7	17	5	9	15
9	16	5	8	6	14
14	9	5	15	11	7

Leo's graph is not accurate.

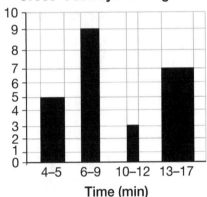

Cross-Country Running Times

1. What is missing from the graph?

_____

2. How is the graph not accurate? Use the Communication Checklist to help you.

_____

_____

3. Sketch a more accurate graph.

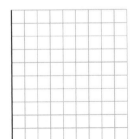

Test Yourself

Circle the correct answer.

1. Paul surveyed 50 boys in his school. He asked them to list their favourite sport.

Sport	Number of boys
Bowling	5
Soccer	32
Curling	3
Cross country running	10

Which group would probably be close to the results of Paul's group?

A. senior citizens   **B.** Grade 5 girls   **C.** parents   **D.** toddlers

2. What are the mode and mean of this group of numbers?

5, 4, 9, 7, 5, 6, 3, 1

A. 5 and 4   **B.** 4 and 5   **C.** 4 and 6   **D.** 5 and 5

3. What is the trend in this broken-line graph?

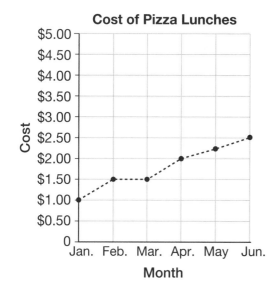

A. gradual decrease in cost   **B.** no change in cost

C. gradual increase in cost   **D.** steep increase in cost

Test Yourself Page 2

Use these data to answer Questions 4, 5, and 6.

Time (min)

20	36	5	49	21	57	36
16	67	16	60	23	44	51
10	21	44	9	46	68	32
63	37	8	68	47	55	19

4. What is the range of the data?

    A. 63   **B.** 61   **C.** 62   **D.** 64

5. What interval would be the best choice to make a bar graph?

    A. 2   **B.** 5   **C.** 8   **D.** 15

6. How many numbers would be in the interval 31–45?

    A. 4   **B.** 6   **C.** 5   **D.** 7

Use the pictograph to answer Questions 7 and 8.

100 students were surveyed about their favourite ride at the fair.

Favourite Rides

Ferris wheel   ☐ ☐ ☐

Bumper cars   ☐

Roller coaster   ☐ ☐ ☐ ☐ ▫

Swing   ☐ ▫

☐ = 12 students

7. What other scale could be used for this pictograph?

    A. ☐ = 10 students   **B.** ☐ = 16 students

    C. ☐ = 15 students   **D.** ☐ = 14 students

8. If the scale were changed to ☐ = 20 students, how would 65 students choosing the roller coaster be shown?

    A. ☐☐   **B.** ☐☐▫   **C.** ☐☐☐▫   **D.** ☐☐☐

1 Adding and Subtracting Using Mental Math

Goal **Use mental math strategies to add and subtract.**

1. Use mental math to calculate each answer.
   Explain your strategy.

   a) 54 + 29 _____

   _____

   _____

   b) 88 + 32 _____

   _____

   c) 100 − 48 _____

   _____

   _____

   d) 70 − 14 _____

   _____

2. The Boston Marathon is a 42 km run. Aaron ran
   the marathon in 100 min.

   | 0 km | 10 km | 20 km |

   0 km   10 km   20 km

   0 min   20 min   40 min

   Use mental math to calculate Aaron's distance
   and time at each point during the 42 km run.
   Describe your strategy.

   _____

   _____

   _____

2 Estimating Sums and Differences

Goal Estimate sums and differences and justify your strategy.

1. Estimate which calculations are reasonable.
   Explain how you estimated.

   a) 2997 + 1158 = 4155

   _____

   _____

   b) 6053 − 4802 = 2251

   _____

   _____

   c) 8095 − 2559 = 5536

   _____

   _____

   d) 3273 + 897 + 4298 = 8238

   _____

> ### At-Home Help
>
> To check the reasonableness of a calculation, estimate the answer using one or more mental math strategies.
>
> For example:
>
> To check if
> 1198 +1510 + 1454 + 1354 = 8516
> is reasonable, use rounding and regrouping. Then estimate the sum.
>
> 1200 +1500 + 1400 + (50 + 1350)
>   = 1200 + 1500 + 1400 + 1400
>   = 5500
>
> So the sum 8516 is not reasonable.

2. The chart shows data for hockey players in a town.

Hockey players		Number of players
Boys	novice level	4854
	atom level	5013
Girls	novice level	3955
	atom level	2081

   How many more hockey players are boys than girls? Estimate to check the reasonableness of your calculation. Show your work and justify your choice of estimation strategies.

3 Adding Whole Numbers

 Goal **Add 3 four-digit whole numbers using paper and pencil.**

1. Estimate and then add. Show your work.

a) 　　2549
　　　　3288
　　　+ 7426
　　　‾‾‾‾‾‾

b) 　　5283
　　　　6094
　　　+ 846
　　　‾‾‾‾‾‾

c) 　　7106
　　　　5882
　　　+ 4037
　　　‾‾‾‾‾‾

d) 1093 + 2764 + 898

e) 7549 + 3808 + 4261

2. Seven students wrote stories, each with a different number of words. What 3 stories have a total between 7000 and 8000 words? Show your work.

Student	Number of words
Raj	2419
Sima	3256
Ben	3780
Cathy	2934
Bill	4087
Dan	2593
Kew	1806

4

Solve Two-Step Problems

Goal **Select operations and solve two-step problems.**

You will need a calculator.

1. Rachel shot baskets each day for a period of
   2 weeks. She shot a total of 2260 baskets. Rachel
   shot 100 more baskets each day during the last
   3 days. How many shots per day did she take during
   the first week?

At-Home Help

When solving word problems,
follow these steps.
- First write down what you are
  asked to find out.
- Then look at the information you
  are given.
- Decide what information is
  important.
- Make a plan.
- Choose operations that use
  the given information to solve
  the problem.
- Check if your answer is reasonable.

Remember to show all your work.

2. Mr. James is 49 years of age. His sister is 45 years
   of age. What is the difference in age in each of
   these units of time? Show your work.

   a) months

   b) weeks

   c) days

3. A school has a total of 1258 students. There are 297 primary students
   and 364 junior students. How many senior students are there?

5 Communicate About a Choice of Calculation Method

 Goal Justify your choice of calculation method and explain each step in solving a problem.

1. Marcus was at Youth Camp. He had a total of 3025 points that he could spend at the camp store. About how many points does he have left?

Camp store item	Cost in points
Candy	875
Ice cream	436
Chips	297
Drinks	980

Alana wrote this rough copy to solve the problem.

> I only need to estimate, because the problem asks "about" how many points are left.
> Marcus spent about 2600 points.
> He had about 3000 points in total.
> He should have about 400 points left.

Write a good copy. Use the Communication Checklist to help you.

At-Home Help

When writing a solution to a word problem, first write a rough copy.
- If the problem does not ask for an exact answer, use estimation to find the answer.
- You can use rounding, regrouping, or any other mental math strategy.
- Check if your answer is reasonable.

Then write a good copy explaining all your steps.

Remember to show all your work.

Communication Checklist
☑ Did you explain your thinking?
☑ Did you show all the steps?
☑ Did you use math language?

2. Richard and his friends collected a total of 4548 old coins. The chart shows some of the coins.

Type of coin	Number of coins
Penny	789
Nickel	1516
Dime	934

a) Richard forgot to list quarters in the chart. About how many quarters were collected?

_____

b) About how many more pennies would be needed to match the number of nickels?

_____

6 Adding Decimals

Goal   Add decimal tenths and hundredths using base ten blocks and pencil and paper.

1. Estimate and then add. Show your work.

a)   8.3
    + 5.7

b)   6.89
    + 5.43

c) 5.16 + 3.87

d) 4.93 + 0.82 + 6.95

At-Home Help

Decimal tenths and hundredths are added using the same rules as whole numbers.

- It is easier to add vertically if the decimal points are aligned.
- Add place values that are the same.
- If the sum of a place value is 10 or more, regroup using the next greater place value.
- Check your answer using estimation.

For example:

		Estimate
	1.76	2
	+ 0.45	+ 0
Actual answer →	2.21	2

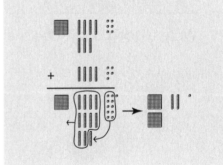

---

2. Estimate and then calculate the total distance. Show your work.

0.85 km and 5.28 km

3. Dmitri added 2.78 and 5.49. He also added 278 and 549. He compared his answers.

a) Explain how the answers are the same.

_____

_____

b) Explain how the answers are different.

_____

_____

Adding Money

 Goal Use various methods to calculate the cost of purchases.

1. Estimate and then add. Show your work.

a) $23.65
     19.88
  + 14.63

b) $18.63
  + 12.88

c) $52.64
      0.86
   + 8.29

At-Home Help

Adding money amounts is the same as adding decimal hundredths.

Use estimation to check your sums.

For example:

		Estimate
	$29.95	$30
	+ 35.95	+ 36
Actual answer →	$65.90	$66

d) $2.65 + $1.74

e) $13.43 + $7.09

f) $48.91 + $0.72

2. a) Create a problem involving buying 2 or more video games. Solve your problem. Show your estimate and actual answer.

Name of video game	Cost
Hockey Super Stars	$26.50
World Cup Soccer	$23.78
Race Car Rally	$10.45
Wave Surfer	$9.99

b) Explain how you calculated your answer. Then check your answer.

Making Change

Goal   **Calculate change from purchases.**

1. Calculate the total cost and the amount of change.

a)

$12.94

$2.53

_____

b)

$14.36

$11.90

$3.89

_____

c)

$36.59

$18.70

_____

d)

$13.98

$39.

$43.65

_____

2. You have been given $60 for your birthday.

   a) Choose 2 items you can buy. Calculate the total cost. Then choose 3 items and calculate the total cost. Show your work.

Item	Cost
Shirt	$25.85
Binder	$15.99
Sunglasses	$9.43
Video game	$17.68
Book	$23.97
Music CD	$34.25

   b) How much change will you receive? Show your work.

Subtracting Decimals

Use base ten blocks and pencil and paper to subtract decimal tenths and hundredths.

1. Estimate and then subtract. Show your work.

a) 9.85   b) 6.03   c) 7.00   d) 8.67
  − 7.14   − 1.57   − 4.96   − 5.82

e) 7.6 − 3.8   f) 9.00 − 5.16   g) 25.34 − 5.79

2. In long jump, Benjamin jumped 4.85 m while his friend Dan jumped 5.62 m. How much farther did Dan jump than Benjamin?

_____

3. Sofia got an answer of 3.75 when she subtracted 5.25 from a whole number. What is the whole number? Explain how you got your answer.

_____

_____

At-Home Help

Decimal tenths and hundredths are subtracted using the same rules as whole numbers.

- It is easier to subtract vertically if the decimal points are aligned.
- Subtract place values that are the same starting from the smallest place value.
- If you can't find the difference for a particular place value, regroup using the next greater place value.
- Check your answer using estimation.

For example:

		Estimate
	3.00	3
	− 0.75	− 1
Actual answer →	2.25	2

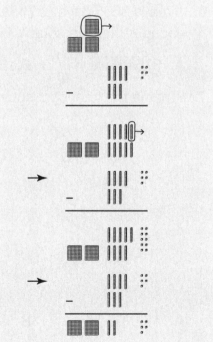

Test Yourself

Circle the correct answer.

1. Which question would give an answer close to 2591?

   A. 3658 − 1149   **B.** 1468 + 1897   **C.** 1255 + 1349   **D.** 4513 − 2928

2. Using estimation, which question has an answer between 1350 and 1450?

   A. 1046 + 829   **B.** 6391 − 4869   **C.** 874 + 573   **D.** 2836 − 1264

3. Which calculation is correct?

   A. 1259 + 745 + 5567 = 7754   **B.** 1259 + 745 + 5567 = 6747

   C. 1259 + 745 + 5567 = 6574   **D.** 1259 + 745 + 5567 = 7571

4. Three transport trucks can move loads that total 4581 kg. Two of the trucks moved 2614 kg and 1088 kg. How much would you estimate the third truck moved?

   A. 780 kg   **B.** 700 kg   **C.** 900 kg   **D.** 800 kg

5. What is the answer to 7246 − 3859?

   A. 4613   **B.** 3387   **C.** 4631   **D.** 3287

6. Sima is 3655 days old. Mario's cousin is 298 days older than Sima. Mario is 189 days younger than his cousin. How many days old is Mario?

   A. 3764 days   **B.** 3953 days   **C.** 3466 days   **D.** 3769 days

7. What is the total cost shown?

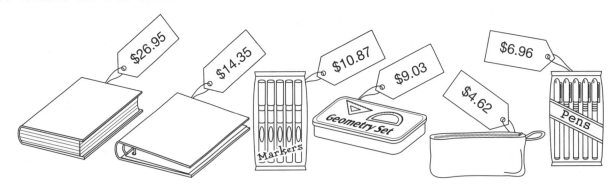

   A. $72.87   **B.** $67.78   **C.** $72.78   **D.** $67.87

8. Tina gave the store clerk a $100 bill for all the items in Question 7. How much change would she receive?

   A. $32.78   **B.** $27.78   **C.** $32.22   **D.** $27.22

1

Using Measurements to Describe Objects

Goal Use logical reasoning to choose measurements.

You will need a ruler marked in millimetres.

Fill in the blanks with the correct measurements.

At-Home Help

Measurements can be used
to describe objects. To solve
measurement problems, use the
clues given and your own knowledge.

1 cm = 10 mm
100 cm = 1 m
1000 mm = 1 m

1. Anna's kitchen table seats _____ people.

   It is _____ cm wide, _____ m long,

   and _____ mm high.

   1.5   750   6   90

2. Tilo can cycle _____ km in one hour. The library is 5 km from his

   home. It will take Tilo about _____ min to cycle from home to the

   library. The speed limit for cars on city streets is _____ km/h.

   This is _____ times Tilo's speed.

   5   10   50   30

   MAXIMUM

   50

   km/h

3. A box of crackers is _____ m high, _____ cm deep, and

   _____ mm wide. The box holds about _____ crackers.

   0.18   70   140   6

   Crispy
   Crackers

4. A new pencil is _____ m long and _____ mm wide.

   The eraser is _____ cm long.

   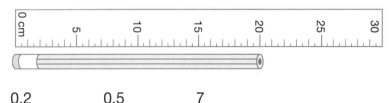

   0.2   0.5   7

CHAPTER 5

2 Measuring Lengths

Goal **Relate metric units of length to each other.**

You will need a ruler marked in millimetres.

1. Describe how you can use a 30 cm ruler to measure ribbon for each length.

   a) 0.3 m _____

   _____

   b) 105 cm _____

   _____

   c) 750 mm _____

   _____

At-Home Help

When measuring objects, you may have to use tools that are available rather than ideal. You can use a 30 cm ruler to measure many lengths.

1 m = 100 cm
1 m = 1000 mm
1 cm = 10 mm

2. Describe how to cut a piece of fabric 0.9 m long using a 30 cm ruler.

   _____

3. Draw each length.

   a) 112 mm

   b) a 0.3 m zigzag path

4. How can you calculate the thickness of one penny in millimetres? Use the information in the picture and a calculator.

   _____

   _____

   _____

5. Two adjacent houses on a street are 1300 cm apart.

   a) Do you think the houses are in a rural or an urban area? Explain.

   _____

   b) What would be a better unit for describing the distance? Why?

   _____

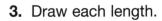
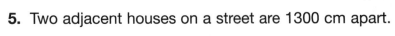

3

Measuring Circumference

 Goal   **Measure around circular objects.**

You will need a ruler marked in millimetres, and a tape measure.

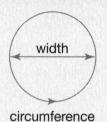
1. Measure and record the width and circumference of each circle in centimetres. Complete the table.

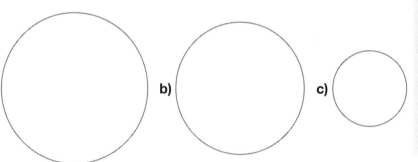

a) b) c)

Circle	Width	Circumference
a)		
b)		
c)		

2. For each circle, is the circumference closer to two times, three times, or four times the width?

_____

3. Liam is practicing for a 400 m race. If he runs around a circular track with a width of 100 m, will he run as far as the race distance? Explain.

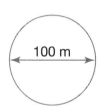

100 m

_____

_____

4. The hula hoops in the gym are 96 cm in width. What is the best estimate of their circumference?

   3 m   270 cm   4000 mm

_____

Measuring Perimeter

Goal   Measure perimeter on a grid.

You will need a metric ruler.

1. The initials for the Maple Leafs are shaded on the grid below. Estimate the perimeter. Check by measuring.

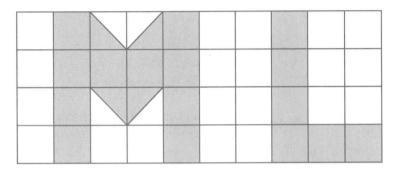

	Estimated perimeter	Actual perimeter
M		
L		
total		

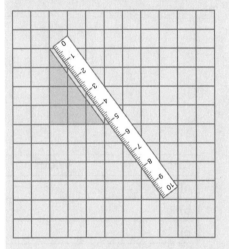
2. Use the grid to draw two different shapes each with a perimeter of 16 cm. Each shape must have more than 4 sides.

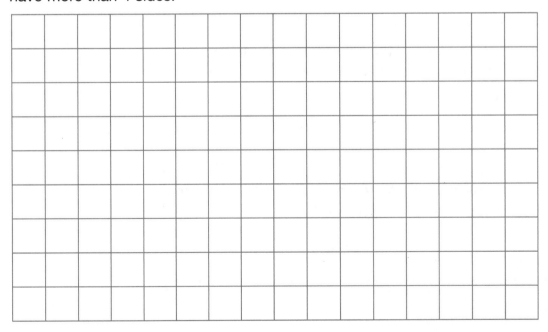

5 Measuring the Perimeter of a Rectangle

Goal **Develop and use a rule for calculating the perimeter of a rectangle.**

1. Calculate the length of trim you would need to go around these blankets.

a)

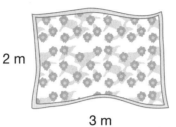

2 m

3 m

b)

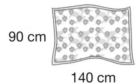

90 cm

140 cm

At–Home Help

In a rectangle, opposite sides are the same length. The perimeter of a rectangle can be calculated by adding the length and width, and then doubling the sum.

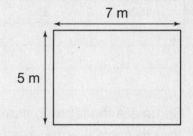

7 m

5 m

For example:

perimeter of this rectangle
= two times (5 m + 7 m)
= two times (12 m)
= 24 m

2. Which rectangle has the greater perimeter? How much greater is it?

a) 7.5 cm by 6 cm   **b)** 7 cm by 7 cm

Rectangle _____ has the greater perimeter. It is _____ greater than _____.

3. a) How will the perimeter of this rectangle change if you add 4 m to the width?

The perimeter _____.

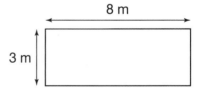

8 m

3 m

b) How will the perimeter change if you divide the length in half?

The perimeter _____.

4. To calculate the perimeter of a square, Sue multiplies the width by 4. Is her rule correct? Explain.

_____

_____

6 Solve Problems Using Tables

Goal Use tables to solve distance problems.

1. Tom cycles 150 m in one minute. He multiplies this by 10 then makes a table of his distances and times.

Distance (m)	Time (min)
1500	10
3000	20
4500	30

At-Home Help

Organizing data in tables helps you see patterns. Using tables is an effective problem-solving strategy.

For example, as the distance increases by 1000 m, the time increases by 10 minutes.

Distance (m)	Time (min)
1000	10
2000	20
3000	30

Complete the table to estimate how long it will take Tom to cycle 8 km.

It will take Tom about _____ to cycle 8 km.

2. Rosa can paddle her kayak at the rate of 1 km every 5 minutes. At this rate how far will she paddle in 1 hour? Make a table to help you.

3. Tamara skates 120 m in one minute. Emma skates 1 km in 10 minutes. Create 2 tables to find out which girl can skate farther in 30 minutes. How much farther?

7 Measuring Time

Goal **Estimate and measure time to the nearest second.**

1. Juanita is making popcorn. Estimate and then calculate the time it took to make the popcorn.

start   finish

I estimate the time to be _____.

I calculate the time to be _____.

2. Kevin wonders how long the songs on the radio are. He noted the start and end times of one song. Estimate and then calculate the time.

start   finish

I estimate the time to be _____.

I calculate the time to be _____.

At-Home Help

This clock shows when the traffic light turned red.

This clock shows when the traffic light turned green.

The traffic light was red for 1 min 43 s. From 8:47:29 to 8:48:00 is 31 s. From 8:48:00 to 8:49:00 is 1 min. From 8:49:00 to 8:49:12 is 12 s. So the total time was 1 min 43 s.

3. A ride at the amusement park has a sign saying: "Five minutes of thrills and spills!"

Five minutes of thrills and spills!

Yoshi noted the start time of 11:55:26 and the finish time of 12:00:12. Was the sign accurate? Explain.

_____

_____

4. The school bell rings at 9:00:00. How much time is left before the bell?

_____

Recording Dates and Times

Goal Write dates and times using numeric format.

1. Colin's flight home landed on March 25, 2004, at 23 minutes 12 seconds after eight o'clock in the evening.

   Record the date and time in numeric format.

   _____

2. Colin departed three weeks before his return home at five minutes after noon.

   Record his departure time in numeric format.

   _____

3. Write each birth date and time in numeric format.

   a) July 18, 1999 at 3 minutes 15 seconds after midnight

   _____

   b) November 20, 2001 at 4 seconds after six thirty in the evening

   _____

4. The Internet Café charges $0.50 for each minute or part of a minute. How much should Sofie pay if she logs on at 16:48:33 and logs off at 17:00:26? Show your work.

At-Home Help

When dates are recorded in numeric format, the year is recorded first, then a hyphen, then the month (using two digits), then another hyphen, then the day (using two digits).

For example, March 10, 2004 would be written as 2004-03-10.

The times on flight, train, and ship schedules are recorded using a 24 hour clock. The hour is written first, followed by a colon, then the minute(s), also followed by a colon, then the seconds (all numbers must have two digits).

On a 24 hour clock, noon is written as 12:00:00. On digital clocks, midnight is displayed as 00:00:00. All hours are written according to the number of hours after midnight.

For example, 1 p.m. is written as 13:00:00.

Test Yourself

Circle the correct answer.

1. A student desk is about _____ m high. It measures about _____ mm across and about _____ cm from front to back. What are the measurements?

   A. 0.8, 650, 410   **B.** 80, 650, 41

   C. 0.8, 65, 41   **D.** 0.8, 650, 41

2. What is the thickness of 1 floppy disk in mm? Use the information in the picture to help you.

   15 floppy disks

   3 cm

   A. 2   **B.** 30

   C. 3   **D.** 20

3. The width of Adam's bicycle wheel is 0.6 m. What is the best estimate of the circumference of the wheel?

   A. 60 cm   **B.** 1.2 m   **C.** 2.5 m   **D.** 190 cm

4. What is the perimeter of this shape?

   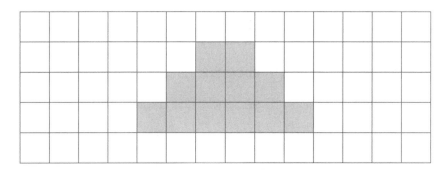

   A. 14 cm   **B.** 18 cm   **C.** 12 cm   **D.** 20 cm

5. A 7.5 cm by 6 cm photo is enlarged. The length and the width are doubled. What is the perimeter of the new photo?

   A. 7.5 cm greater   **B.** double the original perimeter

   C. 12 cm greater   **D.** 1.5 times the original perimeter

6. Fiona rides her skateboard about 150 m in 1 minute. She made a table to track her distance and time. About how long will it take her to skateboard 4 km?

Distance (m)	Time (min)
1500	10
3000	20

A. 20 minutes

B. 23 minutes

C. 27 minutes

D. 30 minutes

7. Neil wants to synchronize the clocks in his home. When the radio announced it was exactly noon, three clocks in his home looked like this:

How must Neil correct the time on each clock?

A. (i) back 23 seconds, (ii) ahead 1 minute 44 seconds, (iii) back 2 minutes

B. (i) back 37 seconds, (ii) ahead 1 minute 44 seconds, (iii) back 2 minutes

C. (i) back 37 seconds, (ii) ahead 1 minute 16 seconds, (iii) back 2 minutes

D. (i) ahead 37 seconds, (ii) ahead 2 minutes 44 seconds, (iii) back 2 minutes

8. A hot air balloon will be launched at 40 minutes 30 seconds after 3 p.m. on Canada Day (July 1), 2007. How would the date and time of the launch be written in numeric format?

A. 2007-01-07 3:40:30

B. 2007-01-07 03:40:30

C. 2007-07-01 15:40:30

D. 2007-01-07 15:40:30

9. Which statement best describes circumference?

A. Circumference is the distance around a circle.

B. Circumference is the width of a circle.

C. Circumference is the distance around any object.

D. Circumference is the area of a circle.

1 Multiplying Tens

Goal   Use number facts to multiply by tens.

1. What number facts can you use to calculate these answers? Find the answers.

	Number fact	Answer
a) 40 × 30	_____	_____
b) 50 × 70	_____	_____
c) 60 × 20	_____	_____
d) 90 × 80	_____	_____

2. How can you use this array to calculate 30 × 60? Find the product.

3. Use the array to multiply 40 × 20.

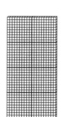

At-Home Help

A **product** is the answer to a multiplication question.

For example, 66 is the product of 11 × 6.

11 × 6 = 66

When you multiply tens, it is easier to use multiplication facts for the non-zero digits.

For example, to multiply 30 × 20 use the multiplication fact 3 × 2 = 6.

An array can help with multiplication.

30 × 20 = 600

---

4. Calculate the area of each rectangle.

a)

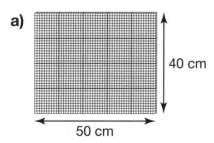

40 cm

50 cm

b)

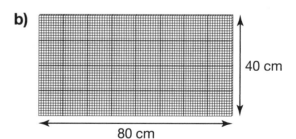

40 cm

80 cm

5. Calculate each product. Explain your thinking.

Explanation

a) 30 × 60 = _____   _____

b) 70 × 40 = _____   _____

CHAPTER 6

2 Estimating Products

Goal Solve two-step problems and use estimation to check the reasonableness of a calculation.

1. Estimate which calculations are reasonable. Explain how you estimated.

   a) 224 × 8 = 1792

   _____

   _____

   b) 29 × 58 = 1200

   _____

   _____

   c) 1475 × 99 = 213 425

   _____

   d) 49 × 49 = 2401

   _____

> ### At-Home Help
>
> To check the reasonableness of a multiplication, estimate the answer by rounding the numbers being multiplied to the nearest 10.
>
> For example:
>
> To check if 12 × 39 = 468 is reasonable, round 12 and 39 to the nearest ten. Then multiply.
> 10 × 40 = 400
>
> So the product 468 is reasonable.

2. Trevor has 60 nickels and 50 dimes. He wants to know if he can buy a CD that costs $11.55. How much more money does he need to buy the CD? Explain how you solved the problem.

   _____

   _____

3. A group of 25 hockey players are having a contest to see who can sell the most chocolate bars. Each group of 5 players gets a box of 30 chocolate bars.

   a) Calculate the greatest number of chocolate bars that can be sold. Show your work.

   b) Use estimation to show that your calculation in Part **a)** is reasonable. Explain your thinking.

3 Solve Problems Using Tree Diagrams

 Goal Use a tree diagram to solve combination problems.

Norman is designing hats for his baseball team.
The designs include 3 colours, 2 logos, and 3 styles.

Colour	Logo	Style
Blue	Maple leaf	Button with stitching
Red	Baseball bat and ball	Button with no stitching
Black		Smooth top

1. How many different baseball hats can Norman design? Use a tree diagram.

At-Home Help

To find the number of combinations of items in a problem, use a tree diagram to list all possibilities.

Choose one item and list all the combinations for it. Repeat this process for all items.

For example, if you have 3 types of hats, 2 fabrics, and 4 colours, then the total number of different hats you can make is 24.

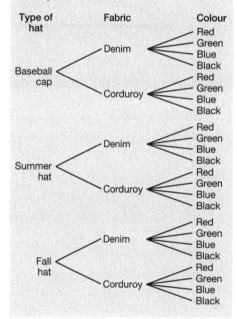

2. Create a tree diagram using 2 colours and 2 logos to get a total of 4 different hats.

Multiplying by Regrouping

Goal Use mental math to multiply two two-digit numbers.

1. Use each number line to calculate.

   a) 12 × 14 = _____

   b) 15 × 11 = _____

   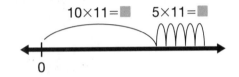

At-Home Help

Regrouping is a mental math strategy for multiplying numbers. Regroup numbers into 10s to make calculations easier.

For example:

12 × 12 can be regrouped as (10 + 2) × 12. 10 × 12 = 120 and 2 × 12 = 24.

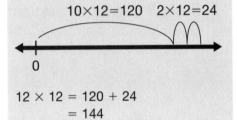

12 × 12 = 120 + 24
= 144

2. Use mental math to calculate.

   a) 12 × 16 = _____

   b) 17 × 11 = _____

3. Calculate.

   a) 11 × 12 = _____

   b) 12 × 18 = _____

   c) 15 × 13 = _____

4. A roller coaster holds 15 people. How many people can go on the roller coaster in 22 rides?

5. How many cobs of corn are in 19 dozen?

Multiplying with Arrays

Goal **Multiply two-digit numbers.**

1. Calculate the number of cells in each table.

   a) 11 rows and 13 columns _____

   b) 17 rows and 21 columns _____

   c) 13 rows and 15 columns _____

2. What multiplication question is represented by these base ten blocks? Calculate the product.

   a)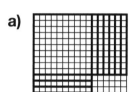

   b)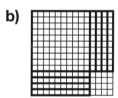

   c)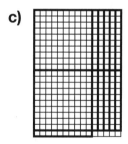

At-Home Help

Arrays of base ten blocks can help when multiplying two numbers.

Represent one number vertically. Represent the second number horizontally. Place enough blocks to complete the rectangle.

For example, 19×23 would look like

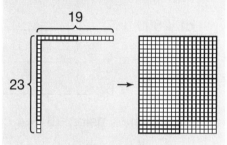

To multiply, find the product of each section. Then add to find the answer.

$20 \times 10 = 200$, $3 \times 10 = 30$,
$20 \times 9 = 180$, and $3 \times 9 = 27$

$$19 \times 23 = 200 + 30 + 180 + 27$$
$$= 437$$

or

$$
\begin{array}{r}
19 \\
\times 23 \\
\hline
57 \\
380 \\
\hline
437
\end{array}
$$

3. A quilt has 11 rows and 17 columns of squares. How many squares are on the quilt?

4. Two quilts are made of square patches each measuring 1 dm by 1 dm. What is the area of each quilt?

   a) 14 rows and 18 columns _____

   b) 22 rows and 25 columns _____

6 Dividing Hundreds by One-Digit Numbers

Goal Use division facts to divide hundreds.

1. What division facts can you use to calculate these answers? Find the answers.

	Division fact	Answer
a) $800 \div 2$	_____	_____
b) $1500 \div 5$	_____	_____
c) $1200 \div 3$	_____	_____
d) $2800 \div 7$	_____	_____
e) $3600 \div 4$	_____	_____
f) $4200 \div 6$	_____	_____

2. Explain how using $16 \div 4$ can help you divide 1600 by 4.

_____

_____

3. Explain how multiplication can help you check your answer to Question 2.

_____

4. An 1800 m track is divided equally into 6 shorter runs. Use a division fact to predict the length of each short run. Use base ten blocks to check your prediction.

At-Home Help

To divide hundreds by one digit, it is easier to use division facts for the non-zero digits.

For example, to divide $1200 \div 2$ use the division fact $12 \div 2 = 6$.

An array can help with division.

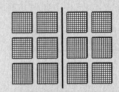

$1200 \div 2 = 600$

You can also check your answer using multiplication.

$600 \times 2 = 1200$

Estimating Quotients

Goal **Overestimate and underestimate when dividing.**

1. Overestimate each division. Show the numbers you used to estimate.

Overestimate

a) 1427 ÷ 5 _____

b) 8)2394 _____

c) 3)1713 _____

d) 5406 ÷ 7 _____

2. Underestimate each division. Show the numbers you used to estimate.

Underestimate

a) 1135 ÷ 2 _____

b) 1303 ÷ 4 _____

c) 2645 ÷ 3 _____

d) 4495 ÷ 6 _____

3. For each question, is it more accurate to overestimate or underestimate? Explain.

a) 2914 ÷ 5 _____

_____

b) 3759 ÷ 6 _____

4. Estimate to solve each problem. Explain your thinking.

a) The total attendance at 2 hockey games in March was 9498 people. Approximately what was the average attendance at each game?

_____

b) Four CDs cost $52.39. Three DVDs cost $48.45. Which item costs more?

_____

_____

At-Home Help
A **quotient** is the answer to a division question.
For example, 8 is the quotient of 48 ÷ 6.
48 ÷ 6 = 8
To do some calculations, it is easier to overestimate and underestimate. The actual answer will be somewhere between both estimates.
With other calculations, either an overestimate or an underestimate gives a fairly accurate answer.
For example, 4753 ÷ 6 would be 4800 ÷ 6 = 800 as an overestimate. 800 is fairly accurate because 4753 is closer to 4800 than 4200.
1095 ÷ 2 would be 1000 ÷ 2 = 500 as an underestimate. 500 is fairly accurate because 1095 is closer to 1000 than 1200.
4539 ÷ 6 would be 4200 ÷ 6 = 700 as an underestimate and 4800 ÷ 6 = 800 as an overestimate. The actual answer is about 750, or halfway between 700 and 800.

8 Dividing Greater Numbers

Goal **Divide a four-digit number by a one-digit number.**

1. Estimate and then divide. Show your work.

	Estimate	Answer
a) $2641 \div 2$	_____	_____
b) $3\overline{)2001}$	_____	_____
c) $6\overline{)3517}$	_____	_____
d) $2134 \div 9$	_____	_____
e) $6\overline{)1604}$	_____	_____
f) $4395 \div 5$	_____	_____

2. Check two of the answers in Question 1 using multiplication and addition.

3. Eight dolphins in a pod each have about the same mass. Their total mass is about 1195 kg. What is the approximate mass of each dolphin?

4. Four trucks are ready to transport the 8 dolphins to a marine centre. Each truck can carry 225 kg. Can the trucks carry all the dolphins in one trip? Explain.

At-Home Help

To divide some numbers, you may need to regroup first.

For example, to divide $1855 \div 4$, use base ten blocks.

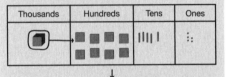

Thousands	Hundreds	Tens	Ones

Thousands	Hundreds	Tens	Ones

Thousands	Hundreds	Tens	Ones

$1855 \div 4 = 463$ R3

9 Choosing Multiplication and Division Methods

Goal Choose and justify a calculation method.

Answer each question using the information given. Explain why you chose multiplication or division.

Did you know...

- the giant Canada goose has a mass of 7 kg
- it flies at a maximum altitude of 245 m from the ground
- it takes 30 days to hatch one nest of eggs
- it can fly about 40 km in 1 hour
- it can fly for about 16 hours each day

At-Home Help

To decide whether to multiply or divide in a problem, look to see if any totals are given.

For example, if the total cost of several items having the same value is given and the problem asks you to find the cost of each item, you need to divide.

If you are asked to find a total, you need to multiply.

For example, if you are given the volume of juice per bottle and the number of bottles, you can find the total volume by multiplying.

1. What would be the mass of a flock of 65 geese?

_____

_____

_____

2. How many hours would the geese have flown in 12 days?

_____

_____

3. How many days would the geese fly if they flew for a total of 592 hours?

_____

_____

4. How many days would a goose sit on 15 nests of eggs?

_____

_____

5. Three geese fly at different altitudes from the ground. They are equal distances apart. Approximately what are the 3 different altitudes from the ground?

_____

_____

Test Yourself

Circle the correct answer.

1. What is the product of 50 × 40?

   A. 900   **B.** 200   **C.** 2000   **D.** 9000

2. What is the product of 90 × 30?

   A. 1200   **B.** 2700   **C.** 120   **D.** 270

3. What is the product of 600 × 60?

   A. 1200   **B.** 3600   **C.** 12 000   **D.** 36 000

4. Which estimate is most reasonable for 26 × 18?

   A. 550   **B.** 450   **C.** 750   **D.** 600

5. Which estimate is most reasonable for 38 × 35?

   A. 900   **B.** 1050   **C.** 1100   **D.** 1200

6. What is the product of 8 × 257?

   A. 2056   **B.** 1656   **C.** 2165   **D.** 2065

7. What is the product of 94 × 62?

   A. 5688   **B.** 5628   **C.** 5828   **D.** 5288

8. What is the area of this rectangle?

   A. 1611 square metres

   B. 1161 square metres

   C. 1616 square metres

   D. 1116 square metres

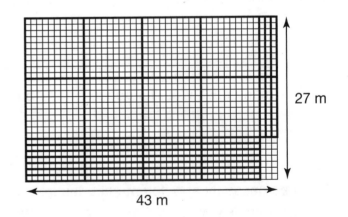

27 m

43 m

Test Yourself Page 2

9. What is the answer to 7396 ÷ 4?

A. 1489   **B.** 1849   **C.** 1949   **D.** 1889

10. What is the answer to 4508 ÷ 8?

A. 563 R1   **B.** 562 R3   **C.** 562 R4   **D.** 563 R4

11. What are the missing numbers from top to bottom?

$$
\begin{array}{r}
57 \\
\times 4? \\
\hline
3?2 \\
2???? \\
\hline
????
\end{array}
$$

A. 4, 6, 280, 2822   **B.** 6, 4, 280, 2622   **C.** 6, 4, 260, 2822   **D.** 4, 6, 260, 2622

12. Tiles are to be placed on a kitchen wall. They are in 18 rows and 14 columns. How many tiles are needed?

A. 254 tiles   **B.** 245 tiles   **C.** 252 tiles   **D.** 225 tiles

13. The area of a rectangular room is 63 square metres. The longest side is 9 m long. What is the perimeter of the room?

A. 32 m   **B.** 30 m   **C.** 31 m   **D.** 33 m

14. A square room has a perimeter of 164 m. What is its area?

A. 1861 square metres   **B.** 1600 square metres

C. 328 square metres   **D.** 1681 square metres

Constructing Symmetrical Shapes

Goal   Construct 2-D shapes with one line of symmetry.

1.

a) Use symmetry to complete the picture.

b) Describe the method you used. Check
for symmetry.

_____

_____

_____

At–Home Help

A line of symmetry may be
horizontal or vertical.

To complete a picture that has a
line of symmetry, use one of these
two ways.
- Use a grid to draw a congruent
  half on the other side of the line
  of symmetry.
- Find matching points by measuring
  the distance from several points
  on the given half to the line of
  symmetry. Make sure distance is
  at right angles to line of symmetry.
  Then join all new points to make
  a congruent half.

Check for symmetry by using one
of these two ways.
- Fold the completed picture along
  the line of symmetry to see if
  both halves match exactly.
- Use a transparent mirror to check
  for congruence of both halves.

2.

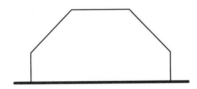

a) Use a different method from Question 1 to complete the picture.

b) Describe the method you used. Check for symmetry and describe your method.

_____

_____

_____

_____

_____

Constructing Triangles

 Goal **Draw triangles with given side lengths and angle measures.**

You will need a ruler and a protractor.

1. Draw a triangle with side lengths of 3 cm and 6 cm. The angle between these two sides is 75°.

2. Draw two different triangles that each have one side length of 6 cm and angles of 125° and 25°.

3. Draw three different triangles that each have one side length of 5 cm and an angle of 60°.

Classifying Triangles by Angles

Goal Investigate angle measures in triangles.

You will need a protractor.

1.

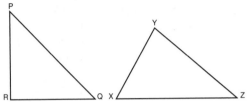

At-Home Help

A **right-angled triangle** has one right angle.

A **right angle** measures 90°.

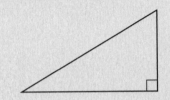

a) Measure and label all the angles in the triangles.

b) Classify the triangles. Give reasons for your answers.

Triangle ABC is _____.

Reason: _____

_____

Triangle PQR is _____.

Reason: _____

_____

Triangle XYZ is _____.

Reason: _____

_____

An **obtuse-angled triangle** has one obtuse angle.

An **obtuse angle** measures greater than 90°.

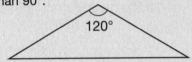

An **acute-angled triangle** has only acute angles.

An **acute angle** measures less than 90°.

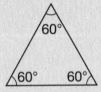

2. a) What type of triangle has an angle that measures 100° and an angle that measures 50°? Give your reasons.

_____

_____

b) What type of triangle has an angle that measures 60° and an angle that measures 90°? Give your reasons.

_____

_____

4

Classifying Triangles by Side Lengths

Goal Investigate side lengths of triangles.

You will need a ruler.

1.

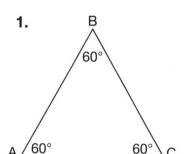

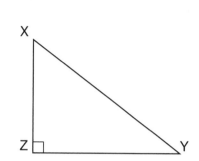

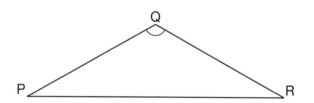

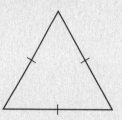
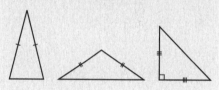
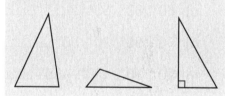
a) Measure and label all the side lengths of the triangles.

b) Classify the triangles according to their side lengths. Give your reasons.

Triangle ABC is ———————————————.

Reason: ———————————————

Triangle PQR is ———————————————.

Reason: ———————————————

Triangle XYZ is ———————————————.

Reason: ———————————————

2. Classify the triangles according to their angle measures and side lengths. Example: Triangle KLM is an obtuse-angled scalene triangle.

a) Triangle ABC is ———————————————.

b) Triangle PQR is ———————————————.

c) Triangle XYZ is ———————————————.

5 Measuring Angles in Polygons

Goal Identify and classify regular polygons by their angle measures.

1. Match these shapes with the angle clues below. Name each shape.

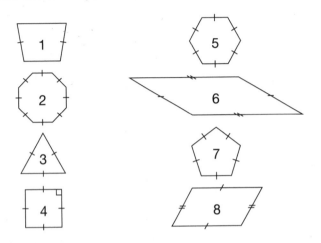

At–Home Help

A **regular polygon** is a polygon with equal angle measures and equal side lengths.

Regular polygons are identified by the number of sides.

The angle measure in a regular polygon increases as the number of sides increases.

For example: Each angle in a regular hexagon is greater than each angle in a square, because a hexagon has 6 sides while a square has only 4 sides.

a) 100°, 100°, 80°, 80° _____

b) 120°, 120°, 60°, 60° _____

c) 60°, 60°, 60° _____

d) 90°, 90°, 90°, 90° _____

e) 30°, 30°, 150°, 150° _____

2. Write angle clues for the remaining polygons. Match the shapes with your angle clues. Name each shape.

Angle clue: _____   Shape: _____

Angle clue: _____   Shape: _____

Angle clue: _____   Shape: _____

3. Without measuring, predict the size of angle A. Use what you know about the relationship between the number of sides and angle measures in a regular polygon.

_____

_____

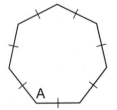

6

Properties of Polygons

Goal Investigate properties of geometric shapes.

1. Match the polygons with the property riddles below.

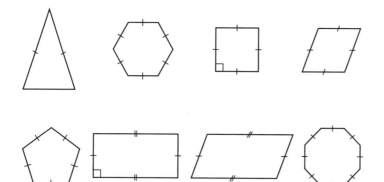

a) I have no parallel sides.
All my sides are equal in length.
All my angles are equal.
I have 5 lines of symmetry.
Who am I?

_____

b) I have 3 pairs of parallel sides.
All my sides are equal in length.
All my angles are obtuse.
I have 6 lines of symmetry.
Who am I?

_____

c) I have 2 pairs of parallel sides.
All my sides are equal in length.
I have 2 pairs of equal angles.
I have 2 lines of symmetry.
Who am I?

_____

d) I have 2 pairs of parallel sides.
My opposite sides are equal in length.
All my angles are equal in size.
I have 2 lines of symmetry.
Who am I?

_____

2. Write property riddles for two of the remaining polygons. Write about parallel sides, side lengths, angle measures, and lines of symmetry. Name each polygon.

a) _____

_____

_____

_____

_____

b) _____

_____

_____

_____

_____

7 Sorting Polygons

Goal Sort and classify polygons by sides, angles, and vertices.

1. Use a Venn diagram to sort these shapes using two of the properties below.
   - number of sides
   - number of angles
   - number of vertices
   - number of lines of symmetry
   - parallel sides
   - equal side lengths
   - equal angles
   - kinds of angles

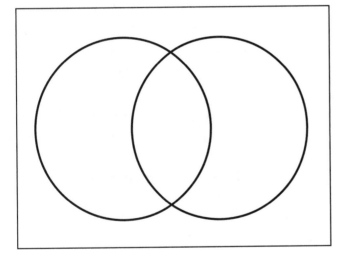

At-Home Help

Polygons can be sorted based on
- number of sides
- number of angles
- number of vertices
- number of lines of symmetry
- parallel sides
- equal side lengths
- equal angles
- kinds of angles

In a polygon, the number of angles and the number of vertices are equal to the number of sides.

An **irregular polygon** is a polygon with different angle measures and different side lengths.

For example:

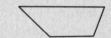

A **Venn diagram** is a drawing with overlapping circles inside a rectangle. This type of diagram is helpful when sorting shapes or numbers.

2. Are there any shapes inside both circles? If so, what properties do these shapes have in common?

_____

_____

3. Are there any shapes outside both circles? If so, why are they placed there?

_____

_____

8

Communicate About Shapes

Goal Use math language to describe geometric ideas.

1.

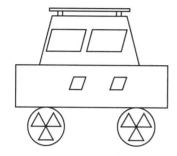

a) Write directions for a friend to draw the picture shown.

b) Use the Communication Checklist to identify the strengths of your directions. List them.

_____

_____

_____

2. If possible, test your directions by having a Grade 6 student use them to draw the picture.

Test Yourself

Circle the correct answer.

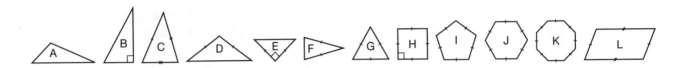

1. Which triangle has no lines of symmetry?

   A. shape A   **B.** shape D   **C.** shape F   **D.** shape G

2. Which shape is a regular polygon?

   A. shape B   **B.** shape C   **C.** shape K   **D.** shape E

3. Which shape has no parallel sides?

   A. shape J   **B.** shape L   **C.** shape H   **D.** shape I

4. Which shape has 2 pairs of equal angles?

   A. shape L   **B.** shape D   **C.** shape H   **D.** shape K

5. Which shape has no obtuse angles?

   A. shape A   **B.** shape K   **C.** shape L   **D.** shape E

6. Which shape is a right-angled isosceles triangle?

   A. shape B   **B.** shape F   **C.** shape E   **D.** shape D

7. Which shape has only acute angles?

   A. shape L   **B.** shape H   **C.** shape C   **D.** shape K

8. Which shape is a scalene triangle?

   A. shape G   **B.** shape A   **C.** shape D   **D.** shape F

9. Which shape is an irregular polygon?

   A. shape L   **B.** shape H   **C.** shape J   **D.** shape I

10. Which shape is symmetrical?

    A. shape B   **B.** shape L   **C.** shape C   **D.** shape D

Areas of Polygons

Goal Estimate and measure the area of polygons.

1. A hockey team chose this logo for their uniforms.

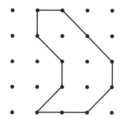

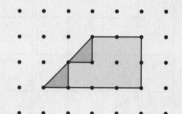
   a) Estimate the area in square units.

   _____

   b) Measure the area in square units.

   _____

2. For each polygon, estimate and then measure the area in square units.

	Estimated area	**Measured area**

a)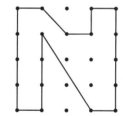

_____ _____

b)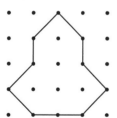

_____ _____

c)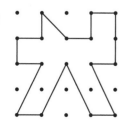

_____ _____

2 Areas of Irregular 2-D Shapes

Goal Develop methods to measure the areas of irregular 2-D shapes.

Find the area of this tulip shape to the nearest square unit using each of the methods below.

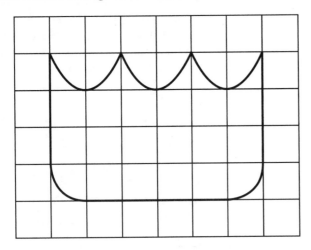

1. Count the full squares. For part squares, if less than half a square is covered, round down. If more than half a square is covered, round up.

   Full squares   **Part squares**   **Total area**

   _____   _____   _____

2. Count the full squares. For part squares, count how many squares you could make by putting together the part squares.

   Full squares   **Part squares**   **Total area**

   _____   _____   _____

3. Count the full squares. For part squares, count only those that are half or more.

   Full squares   **Part squares**   **Total area**

   _____   _____   _____

At-Home Help

A grid is useful when measuring the area of an irregular 2-D shape to the nearest square unit.

On centimetre grid paper, each full square has an area of 1 square centimetre. Part squares that cover less than half a square can be rounded down. Part squares that cover more than half a square can be counted as 1 full square. Part squares can also be grouped to make up about 1 full square.

For example:

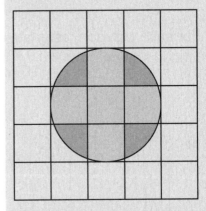

This circle covers 5 full or almost full squares (lightly shaded). There are 4 remaining part squares (darkly shaded), which can be grouped to give about 2 more full squares. So the total area of the circle is about 7 square units.

3 Relating Perimeter and Area of Rectangles

Goal Explore relationships among side lengths, perimeter, and area of rectangles.

Camille has 20 cm of decorative tape to put around the perimeter of a bookmark.

1. Sketch all possible rectangles she can design with a perimeter of 20 cm.

2. Calculate the area of each rectangle in Question 1. Record your answers in the table.

Length of side 1 (cm)	Length of side 2 (cm)	Area (cm²)

3. How are the areas and the shapes of the rectangles related?

_____

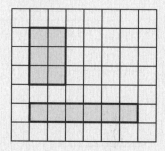

At-Home Help

Perimeter is the distance around a shape. Rectangles with the same area may have different perimeters.

For example:

Both rectangles have an area of 6 cm², but the perimeter of both rectangles is not the same. The top rectangle has a perimeter of 10 cm while the bottom rectangle has a perimeter of 14 cm.

Rectangles with the same perimeter may have different areas.

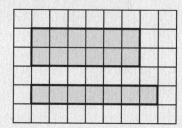

Both rectangles have a perimeter of 16 cm, but the area of both rectangles is not the same. The top rectangle has an area of 12 cm² while the bottom rectangle has an area of 7 cm².

Perimeter is an outside measurement while area is an inside measurement.

4 Area Rule for Rectangles

Goal **Develop and explain a rule for calculating the area of a rectangle.**

1. Jasmine is choosing address labels. Calculate each area. Use the rule for area of a rectangle. Show your work.

a)
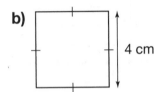
2 cm

8 cm

b)
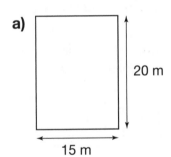
4 cm

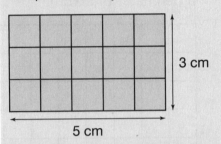
2. Calculate the area of each rectangle. Use the rule for area of a rectangle. Show your work.

a)
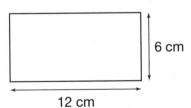
20 m

15 m

b)
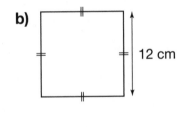
12 cm

3. Nancy is using 1 cm^2 tiles to make rectangular coasters. Each tile costs $0.15. Which coaster will cost the most? Explain.

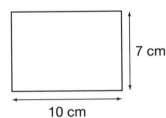
6 cm

12 cm

7 cm

10 cm

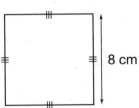
8 cm

5 Solve Problems by Solving Simpler Problems

Goal Solve problems by breaking them into smaller parts.

1. Alain's parents are purchasing new flooring for their living room. The flooring costs $20 for each square metre.

   How much will the flooring cost before taxes?

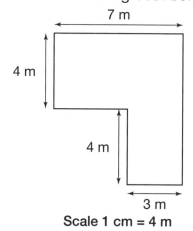

   7 m

   4 m

   4 m

   3 m

   Scale 1 cm = 4 m

   a) Calculate the area by dividing the shape into two parts. Use 2 different sets of rectangles. Did you get the same answer? Explain why or why not.

   _____

   _____

   _____

   b) Calculate the cost of the flooring.

2. A photograph is 12 cm by 16 cm. It has a mount that is 3 cm wide all around it. What is the area of the mount? Show your work.

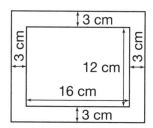

   3 cm

   3 cm

   12 cm

   3 cm

   16 cm

   3 cm

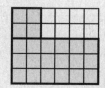
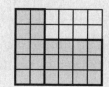
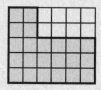

At-Home Help

The area of a complex shape can sometimes be found by dividing it into several smaller parts. The total area is then equal to the sum of the areas of the smaller parts.

For example, the area of this shape can be calculated two ways.

area = area of 2 cm by 2 cm
      square + area of 6 cm by
      3 cm rectangle

   = $2 \times 2 + 6 \times 3$
   = $4 + 18$
   = 22 cm^2

or area = area of 5 cm by 2 cm
        rectangle + area of 4 cm
        by 3 cm rectangle

   = $5 \times 2 + 4 \times 3$
   = $10 + 12$
   = 22 cm^2

Modelling Area

Model area using an appropriate scale.

1. Jasleen's parents are planning a community garden. The dimensions are 20 m by 16 m. They want to make a scale model of the garden on centimetre grid paper.

   a) Choose an appropriate scale. Explain your choice.

   _____

   _____

   _____

   b) Model the garden. Include the scale.

   c) What is the area of the garden? Include the units.

   _____

   d) What is the area of the model? Include the units.

   _____

> **At-Home Help**
>
> Large objects, such as floor plans, towns, and buildings, can be modelled using a scale. A **scale model** may be larger or smaller than the real object but must be the same shape. A scale model is similar to the real object.
>
> When choosing a scale, consider the size of the object and the space you have available for the model.
>
> For example, to draw a model of a 20 m by 12 m patio on the grid below, an appropriate scale would be 1 cm = 4 m. The model will then be 5 cm (20 ÷ 4) by 3 cm (12 ÷ 4).
>
> 20 m
>
> 12 m
>
> Scale 1 cm = 4 m
>
> Remember to always include the scale on your model.

2. Would you measure each area in square kilometres, square metres, square centimetres, or square millimetres?

   a) a restaurant _____

   b) a function key on a calculator _____

   c) a country _____

   d) a postcard _____

Coordinate Grids

 Goal   Use coordinate pairs to identify and describe locations on a grid.

1. Ari drew this logo on a coordinate grid.

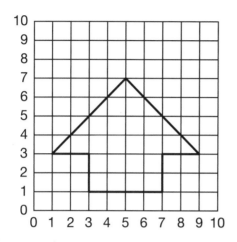

At-Home Help

A **coordinate grid** is a grid with each horizontal and vertical line numbered in order. **Coordinates** identify locations on a coordinate grid, and are sets of numbers that describe where a vertical and a horizontal line meet. The coordinate from the horizontal axis is always written first.

For example, the vertices of the triangle below have coordinates (3, 1), (7, 8), and (10, 2).

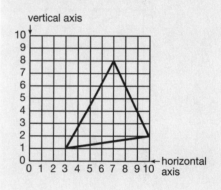

a) What points on the grid could you use to describe the logo? Write the coordinates for each point.

_____

_____

b) Write instructions for drawing the logo from these points.

_____

_____

2. Ken started drawing the initial of his first name on a coordinate grid.

a) Name the coordinates he has used so far.

_____

b) Write the coordinates he would need to finish the letter K. Mark these points on the grid and finish the initial.

_____

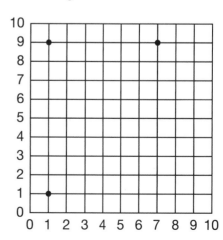

Test Yourself

Circle the correct answer.

1. What is the area of each shape in square units?

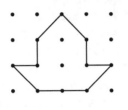 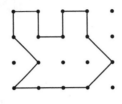

   A. 6 square units, 8 square units

   B. 7 square units, 7 square units

   C. 8 square units, 6 square units

   D. 9 square units, 8.5 square units

2. What is the area of each shape to the nearest square centimetre?

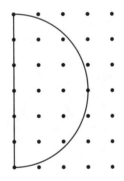 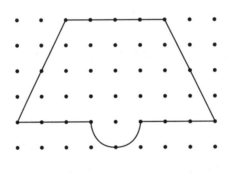

   A. 11 cm^2, 24 cm^2

   B. 14 cm^2, 26 cm^2

   C. 17 cm^2, 24 cm^2

   D. 18 cm^2, 28 cm^2

3. Pat made a rectangle using square stickers. The stickers are 1 cm^2. The perimeter of the rectangle is 22 cm. Of all the rectangles Pat could have made, what are the dimensions of the rectangle with the smallest area and the rectangle with the largest area?

   A. 2 cm by 9 cm, 4 cm by 7 cm

   B. 3 cm by 8 cm, 4 cm by 7 cm

   C. 4 cm by 7 cm, 5 cm by 6 cm

   D. 1 cm by 10 cm, 5 cm by 6 cm

4. A rectangle has an area of 48 cm^2. What dimensions would give the shortest perimeter?

   A. 6 cm by 6 cm   **B.** 6 cm by 8 cm   **C.** 4 cm by 12 cm   **D.** 2 cm by 24 cm

Test Yourself Page 2

5. What is the area of each rectangle?

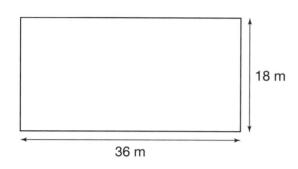

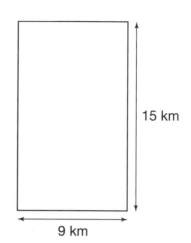

A. 648 cm², 24 cm²

B. 648 m², 135 km²

C. 108 cm², 135 cm²

D. 108 m², 24 km²

6. A zoo has the shape of an 18 km by 12 km rectangle. A scale model of the zoo is shown below. What are the areas of the zoo and the model?

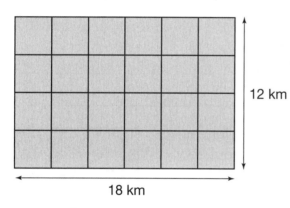

18 km

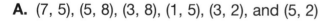

Scale 1 cm = 3 km

A. 60 km², 24 cm²

B. 60 km², 20 cm²

C. 216 km², 20 cm²

D. 216 km², 24 cm²

7. What coordinates would describe this shape?

A. (7, 5), (5, 8), (3, 8), (1, 5), (3, 2), and (5, 2)

B. (5, 7), (8, 5), (8, 3), (1, 5), (3, 2), and (5, 2)

C. (5, 7), (8, 5), (8, 3), (5, 1), (2, 3), and (2, 5)

D. (5, 7), (5, 8), (3, 8), (1, 5), (3, 2) and (5, 2)

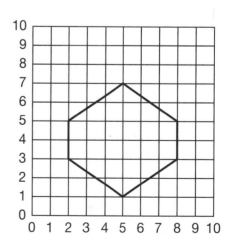

1 Estimating Products

Goal Estimate products of decimal numbers using whole numbers.

1. Each team banner uses 1.9 m of fabric. The fabric costs $7.99 for each metre.

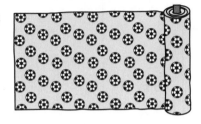

At-Home Help

To estimate decimal products, round each decimal to the nearest whole number. To get a closer estimate
- add a little if you rounded down
- subtract a little if you rounded up

For example:
To calculate 3.7×5.1, round 3.7 up to 4 and 5.1 down to 5. Estimated answer is $4 \times 5 = 20$.

5.1 is closer to 5 than 3.7 is to 4. So to get a closer estimate, subtract a little from 20. Closer estimate is $20 - 2 = 18$.

a) Estimate the number of metres needed for 30 banners.

_____

b) Estimate the cost of fabric for 30 banners.

_____

c) Calculate the cost of fabric for 30 banners using a calculator. Explain why your estimate was higher or lower than the exact amount.

_____

_____

2. Trim for the perimeter of each banner costs $2.89 for each metre. Each banner measures 1.2 m by 1.9 m. About how much will the trim cost for one banner?

1.2 m

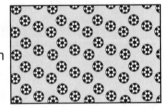

1.9 m

3. Estimate each product using whole numbers.

a) 8×2.6 _____

b) 7.5×1.2 _____

c) $5.1 \times \$4.49$ _____

4. Mark's binder is as long as 16 pennies and as wide as 14 pennies.

What strategy would you use to estimate the dimensions of the binder? Explain.

1.8 cm

2 Multiplying by 10 or 100

Goal **Multiply decimal tenths and hundredths by 10 and 100.**

1. A math text is 2.5 cm thick. How high would a stack of 10 math texts be?

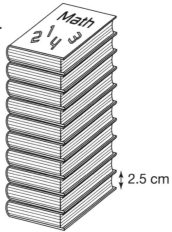

↕ 2.5 cm

2. A box of pencils is 19.5 cm long.

a) How long would 10 boxes placed end to end be?

_____

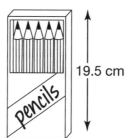

19.5 cm

b) How long would 100 boxes placed end to end be?

_____

3. A package of tennis balls costs $3.79.

$3.79

a) What is the cost of 100 packages? _____

b) What is the cost of 10 packages? _____

4. The mass of a package of tennis balls is 0.45 kg. What would the mass of 10 and 100 boxes be? Circle the correct answer.

| 45 kg, 450 kg | 4.5 kg, 45 kg | 4.5 g, 45 g | 0.45 kg, 4.5 kg |

3 Multiplying Tenths by Whole Numbers

Goal Multiply decimal tenths by whole numbers using models, drawings, and symbols.

You will need base ten blocks and a ruler or tape measure.

1. The mass of a stapler is 0.2 kg. What is the mass of 9 staplers? Draw a representation using base ten blocks.

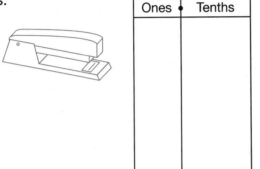

Ones	Tenths

2. Mrs. Gulliver used four 1.7 m pieces of border for a bulletin board. How many metres did she use? Draw a representation using base ten blocks.

1.7 m

Ones	Tenths

3. Rajiv lined up six loonies. Each loonie is 2.5 cm wide. How long is the line of loonies?

◄2.5 cm►

4. Bianca drinks 0.7 L of milk each day. How much milk does she drink in one week?

5. Measure the width of this workbook to the nearest tenth of a centimetre. How long would 6 workbooks be if they were put together side by side?

At-Home Help

When you multiply a whole number by a decimal tenth, it is like multiplying two whole numbers except you have to put in the decimal point because it is tenths.

You can use base ten blocks and estimation before multiplying. If a place value has 10 or more, regroup using the next greater place value.

For example:
$57 \times 2 = 114$
$5.7 \times 2 = 11.4$

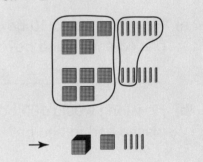

4 Multiplying Hundredths by Whole Numbers

Goal Multiply decimal hundredths by whole numbers using models, drawings, and symbols.

1. Neela ordered 4 tickets. Each ticket cost $4.75.

   a) Calculate the total cost.

   b) How could you have predicted that the cost was less than $20.00? Explain.

   _____

   _____

   _____

2. Multiply. Draw a representation of each question using base ten blocks.

   a) 3.43 × 5   **b)** 6.26 × 2

When you multiply a whole number by a decimal hundredth, it is like multiplying two whole numbers except you have to put in the decimal point because it is hundredths.

You can use base ten blocks and estimation before multiplying. If a place value has 10 or more, regroup using the next greater place value.

For example:
675 × 3 = 2025
6.75 × 3 = 20.25

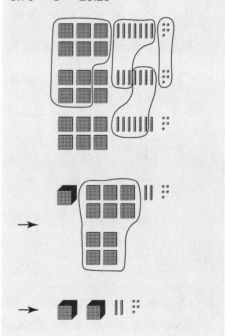

3. Evan cycled 6.68 km. Nadia rode twice as far on her bike. How do you know that Nadia rode more than 13 km?

   _____

   _____

5 Communicate About Estimation Strategies

Goal Explain estimation strategies to determine if a solution is reasonable.

1. Each Canadian dollar is worth $0.76 US. Estimate the cost in US dollars of a software package priced at $30.00 Canadian. Explain your thinking.

_____

_____

_____

2. Use the exchange rate in Question 1. Estimate the cost in US dollars of adult and child admission to the Toronto Zoo. Admission costs in Canadian dollars are $18.00 for adults and $12.00 for children. Explain how you estimated.

Adult admission is about $_____ US.

Child admission is about $_____ US.

_____

_____

_____

_____

_____

_____

> ## At-Home Help
>
> Use the Communication Checklist when explaining and justifying your estimation strategies. You may round or group numbers to make your explanations more clear. You may also want to use models to justify your answer.
>
> For example, to estimate 1.79×8, you may say: "I round 1.79 to 2, then I multiply $2 \times 8 = 16$. I know my estimate is a bit high because I rounded up."
>
> ### Communication Checklist
> ☑ Did you show all your steps?
> ☑ Did you use a model?
> ☑ Did you explain your thinking?

3. One euro is worth about $1.67 Canadian. Tim estimates that a book that costs 25 euros would cost about $30.00 Canadian. Explain how you would decide if this estimate makes sense.

_____

_____

_____

4. A can of apple juice contains 1.36 L of juice. Serina bought 9 cans of juice. What is the best estimate of the amount of juice she bought? Circle the correct answer.

12 L   14 L   9 L   18 L

6 Choosing a Multiplication Method

Goal Justify the choice of a multiplication method.

1. If you know the cost of 10 tiles, how can you calculate the cost of 100 tiles?

_____

2. If you know how much water to add to 1 can of juice concentrate, how can you calculate how much to add to 2 cans?

_____

3. Calculate the cost of 5 kg of each fruit.

   a) Which calculation(s) would you do mentally? Explain your thinking.

   _____
   _____

   b) Which calculation(s) would you do with pencil and paper? Explain your thinking.

   _____
   _____

   c) Which calculation(s) would you do with a calculator? Explain your thinking.

   _____
   _____

> ### At-Home Help
>
> If numbers are simple in a question, you can use mental math. Multiplying by 10 or 100, or multiplying one-digit numbers, can be done mentally.
>
> For example, $\$7.00 \times 8 = \$56.00$.
>
> If you can multiply numbers without a lot of regrouping, use pencil and paper.
>
> For example, $\$5.20 \times 7 = \$36.40$.
>
> If you have to use a lot of regrouping to multiply, use a calculator.
>
> For example, $\$6.47 \times 12 = \$77.64$.

Test Yourself

Circle the correct answer.

1. What whole numbers would be best to estimate the product of 5.7 × $3.35?

   A. 5 × $3   **B.** 5 × $4   **C.** 6 × $3   **D.** 6 × $4

2. Fabric for a flag costs $7.69 for each metre. The flag is 6.3 m long. Vanessa estimated the cost by multiplying 6 × $8 = $48. How would you describe her estimate?

   A. very high   **B.** very low   **C.** close   **D.** high

3. You multiply a decimal number by 10 and the product is 55. What is the decimal number?

   A. 5.5   **B.** 55   **C.** 55.5   **D.** 0.55

4. An insect's image is 1.4 cm in length. It is enlarged to 100 times that length. What is the enlarged length?

   A. 14 cm   **B.** 140 cm   **C.** 14 m   **D.** 1.4 cm

5. A hundreds block represents 1. What multiplication question is modelled here?

   A. 1.7 × 4 = 6.8

   B. 1.7 × 4 = 5.8

   C. 4 × 1.7 = 8.6

   D. 4 × 1.7 = 68

6. A hundreds block represents 1. This arrangement models a multiplication question. It can also show a related multiplication question. What are the two questions?

   A. 4 × 3.5 and 2 × 8

   B. 4 × 3.5 and 7 × 8

   C. 4 × 3.5 and 4 × 7

   D. 4 × 3.5 and 2 × 7

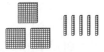
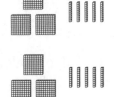

Test Yourself Page 2

7. A binder costs $3.69 and a package of paper costs $1.49. Megan buys 3 binders and 4 packages of paper. What is the total cost before taxes?

   A. $11.07   B. $19.23

   C. $17.03   D. $5.96

8. Serge cycles 0.15 km each minute. How far will he cycle in 12 minutes?

   A. 18 km   B. 1.8 km   C. 180 km   D. 1.5 km

9. Serge has to cycle 5 km. He cycles at a rate of 0.15 km/min. About how long will it take him to cycle 5 km?

   A. about 15 min   B. about 60 min   C. about 30 min   D. about 1.5 h

10. Ed has to calculate these products. He wants to do the calculations efficiently.

   (i) 6.17×11 (ii) 4.10×5 (iii) 5.32×2 (iv) 8.00×8

   What methods should Ed use?

   A. (i) a calculator, (ii) pencil and paper, (iii) pencil and paper, (iv) mentally

   B. (i) mentally, (ii) a calculator, (iii) pencil and paper, (iv) a calculator

   C. (i) pencil and paper, (ii) a calculator, (iii) mentally, (iv) mentally

   D. (i) pencil and paper, (ii) mentally, (iii) mentally, (iv) a calculator

11. A package of stickers costs $3.69. How can you calculate how much 5 packages cost?

   A. Multiply $3.69 by 10.

   B. Divide $3.69 by 10.

   C. Multiply $3.69 by 5.

   D. Divide $3.69 by 5.

1 Estimating Quotients

Goal Estimate quotients when dividing decimal numbers.

Heather is wrapping gifts. She has 5.25 m of ribbon.

1. Heather wants to use this ribbon for 2 gifts. Estimate the length she will use for each gift.

_____

2. She wants to use this ribbon for 3 gifts. Estimate the length she will use for each gift.

_____

3. How could you use your answer to Question 1 to estimate the length needed for 4 gifts?

_____

4. The shortest length of ribbon Heather can use to decorate a gift is about 0.5 m. Does she have enough ribbon to decorate 10 gifts?

_____

2 Dividing by 10

Goal Use regrouping to divide decimal numbers by 10.

1. Craig wants to calculate the length of his running stride. He ran 14.6 m in 10 strides.

   a) Use base ten blocks in a place value chart to calculate the length of Craig's stride.

Tens	Ones	• Tenths	Hundredths

   Craig's stride is _____ long.

   b) Use multiplication to check your answer to Part **a)**.

> **At–Home Help**
>
> When you divide any number by 10, the quotient has the same digits as the dividend but each digit moves to the next lower place value.
>
> For example, using whole numbers, $350 \div 10 = 35$. The 3 hundreds in 350 become 3 tens, the 5 tens become 5 ones, and the 0 ones become 0 tenths.
>
> Using decimal numbers, $67.8 \div 10 = 6.78$. The 6 tens become 6 ones, the 7 ones become 7 tenths, and the 8 tenths become 8 hundredths.

2. A patio is 4.4 m long. It is divided into 10 equal sections for placing flower pots. How wide is each section?

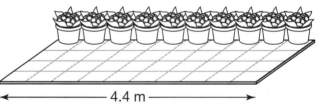

4.4 m

3. A bike rack has sections to park 10 bikes. What is the width of each section if the bike rack is 6.5 m long?

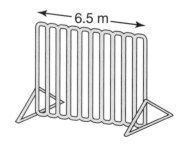

6.5 m

4. Calculate.

   a) $23 \div 10$

   b) $16.9 \div 10$

   c) $66.2 \div 10$

   d) $10\overline{)44.4}$

   e) $10\overline{)239.7}$

   f) $10\overline{)263.1}$

3 Calculating a Decimal Quotient

Goal Express quotients as decimal numbers to tenths or hundredths.

1. Graciela has 6 kg of strawberries to divide equally into 8 bags. Calculate the mass of each bag to 2 decimal places. Show your work.

6 kg

At-Home Help

When you divide numbers, it is sometimes possible to find a quotient to the nearest tenth or hundredth. This is done by regrouping the remaining ones to tenths and any remaining tenths to hundredths.

For example:

```
        2.75
   4)11.00
        8
      ─────
      3.0
      2.8
      ─────
      0.20
      0.20
      ─────
      0.00
```

When 3 ones remain, regroup as 30 tenths.

When 2 tenths remain, regroup as 20 hundredths.

11 ÷ 4 to the nearest hundredth is 2.75.

2. What will be the mass of each bag if the scale measures mass to tenths of a kilogram?

   a) 7 kg divided into 2 bags _____

   b) 4 kg divided into 8 bags _____

3. Calculate to 2 decimal places.

   a) 14 ÷ 8   **b)** 12 ÷ 5   **c)** 4 ÷ 5   **d)** 2 ÷ 8

4. Jacob wants to cut a 22 m length of string into 8 equal pieces. Calculate the length of each piece to 2 decimal places.

CHAPTER 10

4 Dividing Decimals by Whole Numbers

Goal **Divide a decimal by a one-digit whole number using models and symbols.**

1. Sam's garden is 1.5 m by 6 m. He divided it into 4 equal sections.

   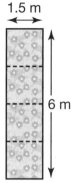

   1.5 m

   6 m

   a) Estimate the area of each section. Show your work.

   b) Calculate the area to two decimal places. Show your work.

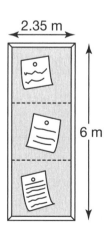

At-Home Help

When you divide a decimal number by a whole number, apply the same rules for division as when you divide two whole numbers. Any whole number remainder is regrouped to tenths and combined with any tenths. Then any remaining tenths are regrouped to hundredths and combined with any hundredths.

For example:

$$
\begin{array}{r}
5.63 \\
4\overline{)22.52} \\
\underline{20} \\
2.5 \\
\underline{2.4} \\
0.12 \\
\underline{0.12} \\
0.00
\end{array}
$$

When 2 ones remain, regroup as 20 tenths and combine with 5 tenths.

When 1 tenth remains, regroup as 10 hundredths and combine with 2 hundredths.

22.52 ÷ 4 to the nearest hundredth is 5.63.

2. Calculate to two decimal places.

   a) 1.98 ÷ 2   **b)** 7.26 ÷ 3

   c) 13.64 ÷ 4   **d)** 5.85 ÷ 5

3. A bulletin board measures 2.35 m by 6 m. It is divided into 3 equal sections. Calculate the area of each section to two decimal places.

4. A hula hoop travels 17.04 m after 6 complete turns.

   a) Estimate the circumference of the hula hoop.

   b) Calculate the circumference of the hoop to the nearest hundredth of a metre.

   c) How far will the hula hoop travel after 4 complete turns?

2.35 m

6 m

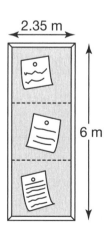

5 Choosing a Calculation Method

Goal **Justify your choice of calculation method.**

Ms Shishido is making origami swans from a sheet of coloured paper. The paper measures 10.5 cm by 46.5 cm. She divides the area into 6 equal parts. Each part has a length of 10.5 cm.

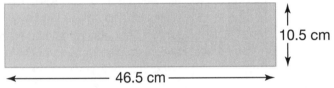

10.5 cm

← —————— 46.5 cm —————— →

At-Home Help

To solve problems, it is important to choose an appropriate calculation method.
- If the numbers are easy to work with, use mental math.
- If the problem asks "About how many …" use estimation.
- If the problem asks for an accurate answer and you cannot easily calculate the numbers in your head, then use paper and pencil or a calculator.

1. About how wide is each part? _____

   To get my answer I used _____

   because _____ .

2. How wide is each part to the nearest hundredth of a centimetre? _____

   To get my answer I used _____ because _____

   _____ .

3. If the coloured paper were divided into 3 equal parts, how wide would each

   part be? _____

   To get my answer I used _____ because _____

   _____ .

4. If 10 swans were made from the coloured paper, what would be the width of

   each part? _____

   To get my answer I used _____ because _____

   _____ .

CHAPTER 10

6 Dividing to Compare

Goal   Use division and other operations to solve problems about money.

You will need a calculator.

1. Vasco, his father, and his grandfather, who is a senior citizen, tour the zoo regularly by bus. Vasco is in Grade 5.

	Single-fare ticket	Book of 5 tickets
Adult	$3.50	$14.00
Senior and student	$2.50	$9.50
Child (12 and under)	$1.25	$4.50

a) What is the cost difference per ticket between a single-fare ticket and a book of tickets? Show your work.

b) How much would each person save by using a book of tickets instead of single-fare tickets? Show your work.

2. A package of 3 energy-efficient light bulbs costs $9.87. A package of 5 bulbs costs $14.95.

a) What is the cost difference per light bulb between the two packages? Show your work.

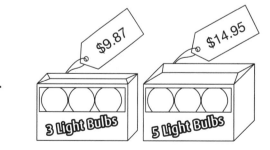

b) If 15 high-efficiency bulbs are purchased, what will be the cost difference between buying them in packages of 3 and packages of 5?

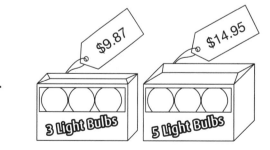

At–Home Help

There are two ways to compare costs if you know the cost of a package of items and the cost of an individual item.

- Find the cost per item in the package by dividing the cost by the number of items.
- Multiply the cost of an individual item by the number of items in the package.

For example:

The cost of a package of 5 tennis balls is $3.95 and the cost of one tennis ball is $1.19.

cost of one tennis ball in package
$$= \$3.95 \div 5$$
$$= \$0.79$$
difference $= \$1.19 - \$0.79$
$$= \$0.40 \text{ per tennis ball}$$
OR

cost of 5 tennis balls
$$= 5 \times \$1.19$$
$$= \$5.95$$
difference $= \$5.95 - \$3.95$
$$= \$2.00 \text{ per 5 tennis balls}$$

It is more expensive to buy the tennis balls individually.

Calculating the Mean

 Use division to calculate the mean.

1. Karen and Fariq play basketball on different teams. Their team scores for last month are shown below.

Karen's team scores	Fariq's team scores
26	37
33	13
17	22
24	

Calculate the mean score for each team.

At-Home Help

The **mean** of a set of numbers is equal to the sum of all the numbers divided by the number of numbers in the set.

For example:

7, 8, 9, 11, 11, 14

$$\text{sum} = 7 + 8 + 9 + 11 + 11 + 14$$
$$= 60$$
$$\text{mean} = 60 \div 6$$
$$= 10$$

2. Calculate the mean of each set of numbers.

   a) 5, 8, 8, 9, 10

   b) 2, 3, 4, 5, 6

   c) 120, 130, 342, 376

   d) 12.4, 11.2, 9.1, 7.7

3. **a)** Create a set of 5 different numbers where the mean is one of the original numbers.

   b) Create a set of 3 different numbers where the mean is not one of the original numbers.

8 Solve Problems by Working Backward

Goal Use a working backward strategy to solve problems.

1. Keisha delivers advertising flyers. He delivered 16 flyers in his own apartment building. Then he divided the remainder into 3 groups of 27 to deliver in nearby buildings.

   a) How many flyers did Keisha have originally?

   b) Draw a diagram as in At-Home Help to show how you solved the problem by working backward.

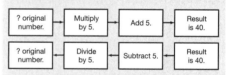
2. Frank collects comic books. He tripled his collection last month. Then his friend gave him 20 more comics. Now he has 68 comics.

   How many comics did Frank have one month ago? Use a working backward strategy. Show your work.

3. A number is multiplied by 8. Then 6.4 is added to the product. The result is 80. What is the original number?

4. Tickets for a concert were sold during the week. 23 were sold on Monday. 30 were sold on Tuesday. On Wednesday 39 were left. How many tickets were there originally?

Test Yourself

Circle the correct answer.

1. A 1.89 L carton of lemonade is shared equally by 6 people. What is the best estimate of each person's share?

   A. 0.3 L   **B.** 0.4 L

   C. 0.5 L   **D.** 0.6 L

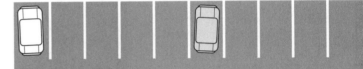

2. Jason's mother drove to work and back, and nowhere else, each day for 5 days. The odometer showed she had driven 95.3 km. What is the distance from her home to her workplace?

   A. 953 m   **B.** 95.30 km   **C.** 9.53 km   **D.** 0.953 km

3. A 45.7 m wide parking lot is divided into 10 parking spaces. What is the width of one parking space?

   A. 457 m   **B.** 45.70 m

   C. 4.57 m   **D.** 0.457 m

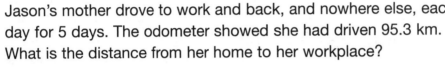

4. A 1.2 kg package of trail mix is shared equally by 8 people. What is the mass of each person's share?

   A. 120 g   **B.** 0.15 kg   **C.** 1.5 kg   **D.** 1.2 kg

5. An open office space measures 24 m by 3.5 m. It is divided into 8 equal-sized cubicles. What is the area of each cubicle?

   A. 84 m²   **B.** 84 cm²   **C.** 105 m²   **D.** 10.5 m²

6. What methods would you use to do these calculations?

   (i) What is the cost of 10 L of gas?

   (ii) About how much would 25 L of gas cost?

   (iii) How much change would Mr. Kwan receive if he paid $40.00 for 25 L of gas?

   A. (i) mental math, (ii) a calculator, (iii) estimation

   B. (i) mental math, (ii) estimation, (iii) a calculator

   C. (i) estimation, (ii) mental math, (iii) a calculator

   D. (i) a calculator, (ii) estimation, (iii) mental math

7. A package of 6 containers of yogurt costs $2.94. Individually these containers cost $0.65. What is the cost difference between purchasing the package and purchasing 6 individually?

   A. $0.96   **B.** $0.16   **C.** $1.96   **D.** $0.80

8. High temperatures for a five-day period were recorded.

Temperature (°C)	17.3°C	18.7°C	14.4°C	19.2°C	11.9°C

   What is the mean high temperature for this period?

   A. 14.4°C   **B.** 16.3°C   **C.** 16°C   **D.** 17.3°C

9. How would you label these statements?

   (i)   The mean of a set of numbers must be one of the original numbers.

   (ii) The mean of a set of numbers can be one of the original numbers.

   (iii) The mean of a set of numbers must lie within the range of the numbers in the set.

   A. (i) true, (ii) false, (iii) true   **B.** (i) false, (ii) true, (iii) false

   C. (i) true, (ii) false, (iii) false   **D.** (i) false, (ii) true, (iii) true

10. A scout group is divided into 6 equal squads. At the last meeting, Squad A had 2 members absent and 7 members present. How many members are in the group altogether?

    A. 42   **B.** 30   **C.** 50   **D.** 54

11. A case of 4 1 L cartons of juice costs $8.96. Individual cartons cost $2.49. What is the cost difference per carton between a case and 4 individual cartons?

    A. $0.25   **B.** $0.30

    C. $0.20   **D.** $0.26

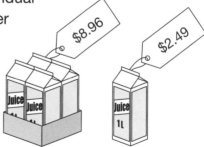

1 Making 3-D Shapes

Goal Draw and build 3-D shapes.

1. **a)** Sketch all the faces of the tent. The base has been drawn for you.

At-Home Help

Steps to draw and build 3-D objects
• Find a model.

• Sketch all the faces.

A pyramid has a base and 3 or more triangular faces.

b) What shape is the base? _____

c) What shape are the other faces? _____

d) Use modelling clay to make the 3-D object. Make the base first and then the faces that join at the top vertex.

e) Draw the model starting with the base. Locate the top vertex and join the vertices.

A prism has a base and top that are congruent, and 3 or more rectangular faces.

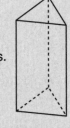

• Use modelling clay to make the object. Always start with the base.
• Draw the model. Always start with the base.

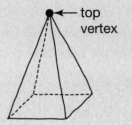

f) What is the shape of the tent?

_____

2. **a)** Draw the faces of a hexagon-based prism.

b) Draw the model of the prism.

2 Making Nets

Goal **Make nets for 3-D shapes.**

1.

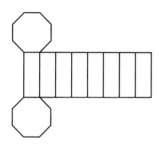

a) Is this the net of a pyramid or a prism? Explain.

_____

_____

_____

_____

b) Name the 3-D object.

_____

c) Draw another net for this object.

d) Trace it on another piece of paper. Cut it out and fold to check.

2. a) Name the 3-D object.

_____

b) Draw a net for this object.

At–Home Help

When you make nets from 3-D objects
• make sure all the faces are traced only once
• make sure the faces are connected in the drawing
• check that the appropriate faces are the same size and shape
• cut out the net and fold to check

This net of a pyramid has triangles attached to the base.

This net of a prism has rectangles all connected. The base and top are congruent, and are attached to opposite sides of the rectangles.

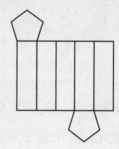

3 Identifying Nets

Goal Match 3-D shapes with their nets.

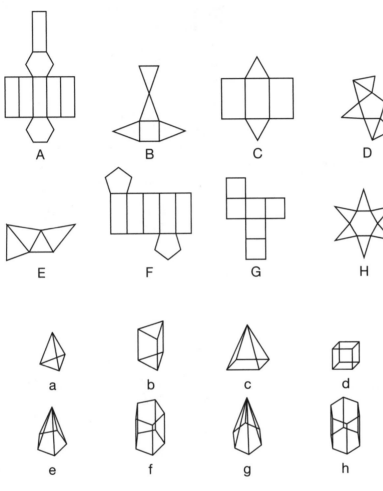

1. **a)** Identify the nets of the pyramids. _____

   b) Explain how you know they are nets of pyramids.

   _____

2. **a)** Identify the nets of the prisms. _____

   b) Explain how you know they are nets of prisms.

   _____

   _____

3. Match each pyramid with its net. _____

4. Match each prism with its net. _____

4 Communicate About Building a Model

 Goal Write clear instructions for building a model from a picture.

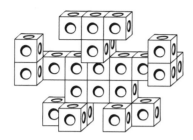

Wendy wrote instructions to make this cube creature.

You will need a whole bunch of cubes.
The head is like a T-shape.
The arms are sticking out, and each arm is 3 cubes.
Each hand is 1 cube, attached to the end of each arm.
The body is flat in the middle.
The legs are short, with 3 cubes each.

1. Go over Wendy's instructions. Revise and improve each line if necessary.

2. Check your instructions using the Communication Checklist.

3. How can you improve your instructions?

5 Measuring and Comparing Capacity

Goal **Estimate, measure, and compare capacities, and determine relationships among units.**

1. **a)** Choose two cups of different sizes in your home. Label them A and B.

   b) Would you use millilitres or litres to measure the capacity of each cup? Write your choices in the chart and explain your thinking.

	Capacity unit
Cup A	
Cup B	

2. Use a big spoon or a soup ladle to compare the capacity of the two cups in Question 1.

   a) Estimate the number of spoonfuls that will fill each cup. Then measure and record the number in the table.

	My estimate: capacity in spoonfuls	Actual capacity in spoonfuls
Cup A		
Cup B		

   b) Which cup has a larger capacity? Explain how you know.

   _____

   _____

   c) Describe another method you could use to compare the capacity of the two cups.

   _____

   _____

   _____

At-Home Help

The **capacity** of a container refers to how much the container can hold. Capacity can be measured using millilitres or litres.

Compare the capacities of two containers using one of these ways.

- Fill each container with water. Then pour the water into a graduated pitcher to measure the capacity. The container with the larger capacity can hold the most liquid.

- Use a spoon or small cup. Record the number of spoonfuls needed to fill each container. The container with the larger capacity can hold the most spoonfuls.
- Fill one container with water. Then pour the water into the other container. If the water overflows, then the first container has a larger capacity. If the water does not fill the container, then the first container has a smaller capacity.

6 Measuring and Comparing Volume

Goal Estimate, measure, and compare volumes using cubic centimetres.

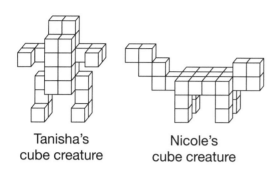

Tanisha's cube creature   Nicole's cube creature

Both creatures were made using centimetre linking cubes.

1. **a)** For Tanisha's creature, count and record the number of cubes in each body part.

At-Home Help

Volume is the space taken up by an object.

To measure the volume of a 3-D object made from centimetre cubes, count the total number of cubes using one of these two ways.
- Count the number of cubes in each section. Then find the total number of cubes for all sections.
- Look at the object from above. Count the number of cubes in each column. Then find the total number of cubes for all columns.

The unit for volume is cubic centimetres (cm^3).

Body part	Number of cubes
head	
body	
2 arms	
2 hands	
2 legs	
2 feet	

b) What is the volume of Tanisha's creature in cubic centimetres? Show your work.

2. **a)** For Nicole's creature, imagine you are looking at the creature from above. Count and record the number of cubes in each column.

0				3					0
1					1				2
0									0

b) What is the volume of Nicole's creature in cubic centimetres? Show your work.

Relating Capacity Units to Volume

Goal Identify the relationship between capacity units and volume units.

 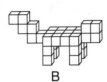 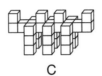

A   B   C

D   E   F

At–Home Help

The units of volume and capacity are related.

$1\ cm^3 = 1\ mL$

The volume of a 3-D object can be measured using water displacement.

- Record the volume of water in the measuring cup at the start.
- Then put the object under water.
- Record the volume of water with the object in the measuring cup.
- The difference between the 2 volumes is equal to the volume of the object.

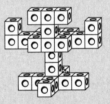

For example, the water level went from 400 mL to 430 mL when this object was put under water. So the volume of the object is 30 mL or 30 cm³.

Models A to F were made using centimetre linking cubes.

1. Find the volume of each model in cubic centimetres. Write your answer below each model.

2. Each of the models A to F was put under water in a measuring cup to measure its volume.

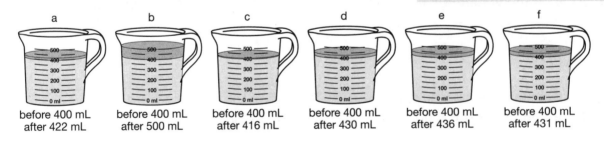

| a | b | c | d | e | f |

before 400 mL after 422 mL | before 400 mL after 500 mL | before 400 mL after 416 mL | before 400 mL after 430 mL | before 400 mL after 436 mL | before 400 mL after 431 mL

Find the capacity of displaced water in millilitres. Write your answer below each measuring cup.

3. Match each model with the correct measuring cup.

Model	Measuring cup
A	
B	
C	
D	
E	
F	

Measuring and Comparing Mass

Goal **Estimate, measure, and compare the masses of objects using appropriate units.**

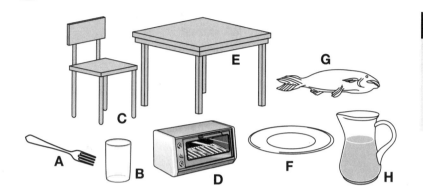

At–Home Help

The mass of most objects we can carry can be measured in grams or kilograms.

1 kg = 1000 g

1. Circle the unit you would use to measure the mass of the objects in the picture.

   A g, kg   **B** g, kg   **C** g, kg   **D** g, kg

   E g, kg   **F** g, kg   **G** g, kg   **H** g, kg

2. Match the masses below with the objects in the picture. There may be more than one possible answer for some masses.

   a) 7 kg _____   **b)** 30 g _____

   c) 10 kg _____   **d)** 150 g _____

   e) 4 kg _____   **f)** 35 kg _____

   g) 250 g _____   **h)** 3 kg _____

3. List three objects you can find in your home that would be best measured in grams.

   _____

   _____

4. List three objects you can find in your home that would be best measured in kilograms.

   _____

   _____

Using Tonnes

Goal **Relate tonnes to kilograms.**

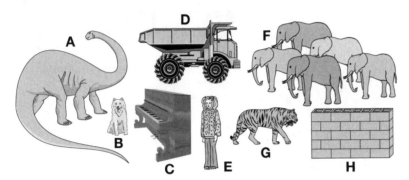

At–Home Help

Objects that are big and heavy, such as trucks, cars, or herds of elephants, are measured in metric tonnes.

A **tonne** is a unit used for measuring mass.

1 t = 1000 kg
1 kg = 1000 g

1. Circle the unit you would use to measure the mass of the animals or objects in the picture.

   A kg, t   **B** kg, t   **C** kg, t   **D** kg, t

   E kg, t   **F** kg, t   **G** kg, t   **H** kg, t

2. Match the masses below with the animals or objects in the picture. There may be more than one possible answer for some masses.

   a) 6 t _____   **b)** 70 t _____

   c) 65 kg _____   **d)** 10 t _____

   e) 45 kg _____   **f)** 150 kg _____

   g) 30 t _____   **h)** 40 kg _____

3. List three other objects that would be best measured in tonnes.

   _____

   _____

Test Yourself

Circle the correct answer.

Models

A   B   C   D   E   F   G

Nets

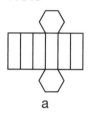   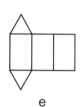 

a   b   c   d   e   f   g

Use the pictures to answer Questions 1 to 5.

1. Which picture is the net of a pyramid?

   A. net e   **B.** net a   **C.** net c   **D.** net f

2. Which net matches with model D?

   A. net b   **B.** net g   **C.** net d   **D.** net c

3. Which model has no parallel edges?

   A. model B   **B.** model G   **C.** model E   **D.** model C

4. Which model has 4 faces?

   A. model F   **B.** model D   **C.** model G   **D.** model A

5. Which model matches with net e?

   A. model A   **B.** model F   **C.** model C   **D.** model E

6. What is the most likely mass for a school backpack?

   A. 2 g   **B.** 2 t   **C.** 50 kg   **D.** 2 kg

7. What is the most likely mass for a piano?

   A. 150 t   **B.** 150 g   **C.** 150 kg   **D.** 15 kg

8. What is the most likely volume for an apple?

   A. 450 cm^3 **B.** 45 cm^3 **C.** 4500 cm^3 **D.** 4 cm^3

9. How much water would likely be displaced if a pencil were put under water?

   A. 150 mL   **B.** 150 L   **C.** 15 L   **D.** 15 mL

Fraction Puzzles

Goal Use patterns to represent the same fraction in different ways.

1. Name the fraction that is shaded and unshaded.

   a) 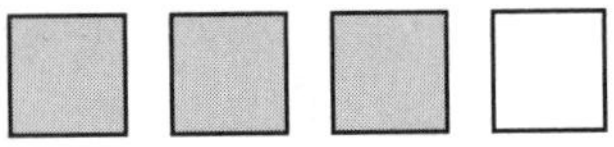 Shaded _____

      Unshaded _____

   b) 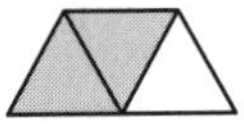 Shaded _____

      Unshaded _____

At–Home Help

Fractions can be represented in different ways.

For example, both pictures show the fraction $\frac{1}{2}$.

2. Represent each fraction on a square.

   a) $\frac{1}{2}$ shaded

   b) $\frac{1}{4}$ shaded

   c) $\frac{2}{5}$ shaded

3. Which square in Question 2 was the most difficult to create? Explain.

_____

_____

4. Make 3 different rectangles where $\frac{3}{4}$ is shaded. Record your results in the chart below.

Number of shaded squares	Total number of squares in rectangle	Picture of shaded rectangle

CHAPTER 12

2

Equivalent Fractions

Goal **Make models of fractions and name equivalent fractions.**

1. Colour each model to show each fraction.

a) $\frac{1}{2}$

b) $\frac{2}{3}$

c) $\frac{4}{8}$

d) $\frac{8}{12}$

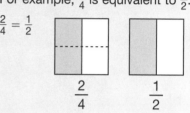

At-Home Help

Equivalent fractions are fractions that represent the same part of a whole or the same part of a set.

For example, $\frac{2}{4}$ is equivalent to $\frac{1}{2}$.

$$\frac{2}{4} = \frac{1}{2}$$

$\frac{2}{4}$ $\frac{1}{2}$

2. Which fractions in Question 1 are equivalent? Explain how you know.

_____

_____

3. Write the fraction to represent the shaded part in each model.

a)

b)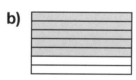

c)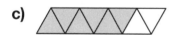

d)

4. Sketch a fraction model that shows an equivalent fraction for Parts **c)** and **d)** in Question 3. Write the equivalent fraction.

c)

d)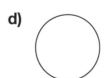

Copyright © 2005 by Nelson Education Ltd.

Comparing Fractions

Goal **Compare the size of fractions.**

1. Compare. Write $>$ or $<$. Explain your strategy.

a) $\frac{3}{8}$ _____ $\frac{5}{8}$

b) $\frac{4}{5}$ _____ $\frac{19}{20}$

c) $\frac{4}{6}$ _____ $\frac{5}{9}$

At-Home Help

Fractions can be compared when the denominators are the same, because the total number of sections and the size of the sections are the same.

For example, to compare $\frac{3}{5}$ and $\frac{4}{5}$, look at the numerators.

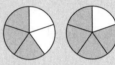

$\frac{4}{5}$ is greater than $\frac{3}{5}$.

If the denominators are not the same, model the fractions using a picture. Then compare the pictures.

For example, to compare $\frac{3}{8}$ and $\frac{2}{6}$ use a model.

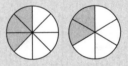

$\frac{3}{8}$ is greater than $\frac{2}{6}$.

2. a) Draw a tablecloth that is $\frac{1}{3}$ red and $\frac{1}{2}$ yellow. Which area is greater? Explain.

b) What fraction of the tablecloth is not shaded? Explain.

Improper Fractions and Mixed Numbers

Goal **Represent and rename improper fractions as mixed numbers.**

1. Draw a picture to represent each improper fraction.

   a) $\frac{14}{4}$

   b) $\frac{15}{10}$

   c) $\frac{12}{8}$

   d) $\frac{7}{2}$

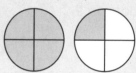

At-Home Help

A **mixed number** is a number made up of a whole number and a fraction.

For example, $1\frac{1}{4}$ is a mixed number.

An **improper fraction** is a fraction with a numerator that is greater than or equal to the denominator.

For example, $\frac{5}{4}$ is an improper fraction.

Mixed numbers can be renamed as improper fractions.

For example, $1\frac{1}{4} = \frac{5}{4}$.

2. Rename each improper fraction in Question 1 as a mixed number.

   a) $\frac{14}{4} =$ _____   b) $\frac{15}{10} =$ _____   c) $\frac{12}{8} =$ _____   d) $\frac{7}{2} =$ _____

3. Change each mixed number to an improper fraction.

   a) $4\frac{1}{2} =$ _____   b) $3\frac{2}{8} =$ _____   c) $1\frac{3}{5} =$ _____

   d) $2\frac{5}{6} =$ _____   e) $5\frac{5}{10} =$ _____   f) $3\frac{4}{12} =$ _____

4. A hockey tournament for younger children is a total of 4 games. Each game is $\frac{2}{3}$ of an hour long. Use improper fractions and mixed numbers to represent each time. Explain your thinking.

   a) length of 1 tournament

   _____

   _____

   b) length of 2 tournaments

   _____

   _____

5 Relating Fractions to Decimals

Goal Use the relationship between decimals and fractions to make comparisons.

You will need a calculator.

At-Home Help

A **decimal equivalent** is a decimal that represents the same part of a whole or part of a set as a fraction. For example:

$\frac{1}{4} = \frac{25}{100}$

$= 0.25$

1. Calculate.

   a) $6 \div 8 =$

   b) $3 \div 20 =$

   c) $8 \div 25 =$

2. Order these fractions from least to greatest. Use inequality signs.

   $\frac{4}{5}, \frac{9}{50}, 3\frac{3}{25}$ _____

3. Write decimal equivalents for each fraction in Question 2.

   a) $\frac{4}{5} =$ b) $\frac{9}{50} =$ c) $3\frac{3}{25} =$

$\frac{5}{100} = 0.05$

4. Order these decimals from greatest to least. Use inequality signs.

   0.20, 1.25, 0.55 _____

5. Write each decimal in Question 4 as a fraction.

   a) $0.20 =$ b) $1.25 =$ c) $0.55 =$

6. Martin won $100 in a bingo game. He shared his prize equally with 8 people in his family.

   a) How much did each person get? Show your work.

   b) How would you write this decimal number as a mixed number?

Solve Problems by Making Models

 Goal Solve fraction problems by making models of the information.

1. Math and reading classes begin at 10:15 a.m. They run for $2\frac{3}{4}$ hours. What time will math and reading finish? Show your work.

At-Home Help

To solve problems with fractions, start by making a model. You may use counters, shapes, or sketches.

You may need to arrange the counters or shapes into groups that match the fractions in the problem.

Use the arrangement to find the answer.

2. Danielle shares her snack with her friends. She has 16 carrots and 12 strawberries. She gives $\frac{1}{2}$ of her carrots and $\frac{2}{3}$ of her strawberries to her friends.

   a) How many carrots and strawberries does she give away? Show your work.

   b) How many carrots and strawberries does she have left for herself? Show your work.

3. Jin fills a container $1\frac{2}{3}$ full while Brad fills a container $\frac{7}{4}$ full. Who has more? How do you know? Show your work.

7 Ordering Fractions on a Number Line

Goal Use number lines to compare and order fractions.

1. Use a number line to find the greatest fraction.

$\dfrac{3}{4}$ $\dfrac{5}{8}$ $\dfrac{4}{6}$ _____

2. Order these fractions from least to greatest.
   Use inequality signs.

   $\dfrac{3}{4}$ $\dfrac{3}{8}$ $\dfrac{5}{6}$ $\dfrac{1}{3}$ $\dfrac{8}{9}$ $\dfrac{1}{2}$

   _____

3. Order these fractions from greatest to least.
   Use inequality signs.

   $\dfrac{2}{4}$ $\dfrac{1}{4}$ $\dfrac{2}{3}$ $\dfrac{7}{8}$ $\dfrac{1}{3}$ $\dfrac{3}{5}$

   _____

At-Home Help

To compare fractions, use a number line to mark the positions of the fractions.

The order of the fractions can be read from the number line.

For example, to order $\dfrac{3}{4}$, $\dfrac{2}{3}$, and $\dfrac{3}{8}$ from least to greatest, use a number line.

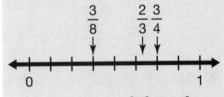

The correct order is $\dfrac{3}{8}$, $\dfrac{2}{3}$, and $\dfrac{3}{4}$.

4. Lise bought different lengths of material to make curtains. She bought $\dfrac{2}{3}$ of a length of silk, $\dfrac{5}{7}$ of cotton, and $\dfrac{4}{5}$ of corduroy. Which material is the greatest length? Show your work.

Test Yourself

Circle the correct answer.

1. What fraction does *not* represent the shaded part of the picture?

   A. $\frac{8}{12}$

   B. $\frac{4}{6}$

   C. $\frac{6}{12}$

   D. $\frac{2}{3}$

2. What fraction is equivalent to $\frac{4}{5}$?

   A. $\frac{2}{3}$ B. $\frac{8}{12}$ C. $\frac{5}{4}$ D. $\frac{8}{10}$

3. Which shaded rectangle is the same as $\frac{6}{9}$?

   A.   B.

   C.   D.

4. What fraction is shaded in the picture?

   A. $\frac{2}{6}$ B. $\frac{8}{10}$

   C. $\frac{2}{3}$ D. $\frac{4}{8}$

5. What fraction is shaded in the picture?

   A. $\frac{2}{3}$ B. $\frac{3}{6}$

   C. $\frac{3}{2}$ D. $\frac{3}{9}$

6. Which fraction is greater than $\frac{5}{9}$?

   A. $\frac{7}{13}$ B. $\frac{6}{10}$ C. $\frac{3}{7}$ D. $\frac{4}{8}$

Test Yourself Page 2

7. Which fraction is less than $\frac{8}{10}$?

   A. $\frac{4}{5}$ **B.** $\frac{8}{9}$ **C.** $\frac{7}{9}$ **D.** $\frac{10}{12}$

8. What is $\frac{14}{8}$ as a mixed number?

   A. $2\frac{6}{8}$ **B.** $2\frac{4}{6}$ **C.** $1\frac{4}{6}$ **D.** $1\frac{6}{8}$

9. What is $\frac{17}{13}$ as a mixed number?

   A. $1\frac{13}{17}$ **B.** $2\frac{4}{17}$ **C.** $1\frac{4}{13}$ **D.** $2\frac{4}{13}$

10. What is $2\frac{3}{5}$ as an improper fraction?

    A. $\frac{13}{5}$ **B.** $\frac{10}{5}$ **C.** $\frac{10}{3}$ **D.** $\frac{8}{5}$

11. What is $5\frac{4}{7}$ as an improper fraction?

    A. $\frac{35}{4}$ **B.** $\frac{54}{7}$ **C.** $\frac{39}{7}$ **D.** $\frac{39}{4}$

12. Which decimal represents the part that is shaded?

    A. 3.5   **B.** 5.3   **C.** 3.05   **D.** 5.03

13. What is the decimal equivalent of $\frac{15}{20}$?

    A. 0.15   **B.** 0.65   **C.** 0.75   **D.** 0.55

14. What is $\frac{17}{20}$ as a decimal?

    A. 0.83   **B.** 0.73   **C.** 0.75   **D.** 0.85

15. What is 0.14 as a fraction?

    A. $\frac{14}{10}$ **B.** $\frac{7}{10}$ **C.** $1\frac{4}{10}$ **D.** $\frac{14}{100}$

16. Raj and Milo play on the same soccer team. Each game is 60 min long. Raj plays $\frac{1}{3}$ of a game. Milo plays $\frac{5}{6}$ of a game. How many more minutes does Milo play than Raj?

    A. 20 min   **B.** 35 min   **C.** 30 min   **D.** 25 min

1 Using Probability Language

Goal   **Use probability language to describe predictions.**

1. Make a check mark under the probability word that would apply for each sentence. For some sentences, more than one probability word may apply. Explain the reason for your choice.

   a) Today is Wednesday.

   b) It will rain today.

   c) The teacher is in the classroom.

   d) The temperature is 1°C and it might snow.

   e) People go on vacation in the summer.

   f) You can travel to another planet in a rocket.

> ### At-Home Help
>
> Probability words are used to describe how likely it is that an event will happen.
>
> Examples of probability words are
> - certain
> - likely
> - more probable
> - less probable
> - impossible

	Impossible	Less probable	More probable	Certain	Reason
a)					
b)					
c)					
d)					
e)					
f)					

2. Which event from Question 1 did you find most difficult to decide the probability? Explain.

   _____

3. Give an example of an event that would fit each probability word.

   a) impossible _____

   b) more probable _____

   c) certain _____

   d) less probable _____

2 Predicting Probabilities

Goal Predict the probability of events and test your predictions.

Letters	Value of each letter
AEIOU	1
LNRST	2
BCDFGHKMPVWY	3
JQXZ	4

At-Home Help

It is possible to predict the probability of an event by repeating an experiment several times.

The results of the experiment can help you think about why the results happened. You can also use the results to predict the probability of other events that are related.

1. Use the information in the table above. Predict how likely each event is.

   a) picking three letters and getting a value of 12

   b) picking a 3-point letter before picking a 1-point letter

   c) picking four consonants before picking any vowels

2. Test each prediction in Question 1. Explain your results.

   a) _____

   _____

   b) _____

   _____

   c) _____

   _____

3. Write the letters from your first and last name on separate pieces of paper. Place them into the same bag or container. Predict how likely each event is. Test your predictions. Remember to place each letter back into the bag after each draw. Explain what you found out.

   a) on the first draw, picking a vowel instead of a consonant

   _____

   _____

   b) on two draws, picking the first letter of your name before any other letter

   _____

   _____

3

Probabilities as Fractions

Goal **Express the likelihood of an event as a fraction.**

You rolled two dice 10 times and recorded the sum of the numbers you got on each roll.

My rolls
12
4
5
10
5
3
7
10
5
9

At-Home Help

When probabilities are written as fractions, the numerator represents the number of likely events, and the denominator represents the total number of events.

For example, if you rolled a die 10 times and you got a 4 three times, the total number of events would be 10, because the die was rolled 10 times. The number of likely events in this case would be 3, because you got a 4 three times. So the probability of you rolling a 4 was $\frac{3}{10}$.

1. Write the probability of each event as a fraction.

   a) getting 5 _____

   b) getting an even number _____

   c) getting a number below 7 _____

   d) getting a number above 9 _____

2. **a)** Write the names of 6 different sports on separate pieces of paper. Place them in a bag or container.

   _____

   b) What is the probability of choosing a sport beginning with letter S? Carry out an experiment. Pick one sport from the bag and record your results. Repeat the experiment 10 times. Write the probability as a fraction.

   _____

   c) Carry out another experiment to find the probability of choosing a sport that has only two syllables. Repeat the experiment 10 times. Write the probability as a fraction.

   _____

4 Modelling Probability Problems

Goal **Conduct probability experiments.**

1. Stefan performed an experiment. He flipped a coin 20 times. The first 10 times he saw heads.

a) Predict the results of the last 10 flips. Write a fraction for your prediction. Explain your prediction.

Prediction   Fraction

_____   _____

Reason

_____

b) Now flip a coin 10 times and record your results in the table. Write your results as a fraction.

Flip of coin	Heads	Tails
1		
2		
3		
4		
5		
6		
7		
8		
9		
10		

At-Home Help

It is possible to predict the probability that an event will happen. To test the prediction, you can do an experiment and record the results in a table.

The results of the experiment can be written as fractions to show probabilities.

Sometimes the results do not match the predictions.

For example, there is a 1 in 2 chance of getting heads when flipping a coin. So the predicted probability is $\frac{1}{2}$.

If you flipped the coin 10 times and got heads 6 times, then the probability of getting heads in the experiment was $\frac{6}{10}$.

2. Write the names of girls and boys on small pieces of paper. Make sure there are 8 names in total. Place the names in a bag or container. Conduct 2 experiments for each part. How many names of girls and boys might give you these results?

a) picking a girl's name is more probable

_____

b) picking a boy's name is very probable

_____

c) picking a girl's name is very improbable but not impossible

_____

Using Tree Diagrams

 Goal   **Use tree diagrams to record the outcomes of an experiment.**

1. Play the game Rock, Paper, Scissors 6 times with a partner at home.

Keep a tally of the results using a tree diagram.

At-Home Help

Tree diagrams are pictures that show all possible combinations for a particular choice.

For example:
A bag has two sizes of marbles. Each size of marble comes in three colours: red, green, and black. There is only one marble of each size and colour. If you were to pick a marble, the choices would be

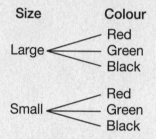

The total number of marbles is 6, and two marbles are red. So the probability of picking a marble that is red is $\frac{2}{6}$.

2. Students choose their pizza slices to eat for lunch. The cost depends upon the type of crust and the number of toppings.

Crust: thin, thick
Toppings: pepperoni, mushroom

a) Draw a tree diagram to show all possible pizza slice combinations.

b) How many different types of pizza slices could you buy? _____

c) Imagine that only one slice is left of each type of pizza, and that you choose a slice by pointing with your eyes closed. Which event is more probable, you choosing a pizza slice with one topping or a slice with two toppings? Record your answer as a fraction. Explain.

_____

_____

6 Solve Problems by Considering All Possibilities

Goal Think about all of the possibilities when solving a problem.

You roll a die and get a number. Then you roll the die again and multiply the first number by the second number. You get 2 bonus points if you make a correct prediction about the product *before* rolling the die the second time.

1. **a)** You play one game and roll a 4 on the first roll. Use a tree diagram to list all possible products.

   b) You play another game and roll a 3 on the first roll. Use a tree diagram to list all possible products.

   c) Based on your tree diagrams, which prediction should you make if you roll 4 on the first roll? Explain.

   _____

   _____

2. Imagine you roll a die 10 times, and record the number you get on each roll. If you were to multiply each number you got by 3, which numbers must you roll to always get a product that is an even number?

Test Yourself

Circle the correct answer.

1. What is the correct order in which to place these probability words?

    A. certain, less probable, impossible, likely, more probable, unlikely

    B. less probable, more probable, likely, unlikely, certain, impossible

    C. impossible, unlikely, less probable, likely, more probable, certain

    D. certain, likely, more probable, less probable, unlikely, impossible

2. Which event is impossible?

    A. It will rain tomorrow.

    B. In Canada, winter is warmer than summer.

    C. We will have a test in math soon.

    D. The school year ends in June.

3. Which event is certain?

    A. I will go to a movie soon.　　　　**B.** I will sleep 8 hours tonight.

    C. Earth orbits around the sun.　　　**D.** All trees will grow this season.

4. Which probability word would best describe this event?

    It will rain 1 out of 7 days this week.

    A. certain　　　**B.** less probable　　　**C.** more probable　　　**D.** impossible

5. Which probability word would best describe this event?

    All students in a class are boys.

    A. certain　　　**B.** less probable　　　**C.** more probable　　　**D.** impossible

6. When Twyla rolled a pair of dice 10 times, these numbers appeared: 10, 6, 9, 10, 5, 3, 6, 4, 6, and 9. What was the probability of Twyla rolling a 6?

    A. $\frac{4}{10}$　　　　　**B.** $\frac{4}{6}$　　　　　**C.** $\frac{3}{6}$　　　　　**D.** $\frac{3}{10}$

7. Look at Question 6. What was the probability of Twyla rolling an even number?

    A. $\frac{6}{10}$　　　　　**B.** $\frac{4}{10}$　　　　　**C.** $\frac{5}{10}$　　　　　**D.** $\frac{7}{10}$

Test Yourself Page 2

8. Look at Question 6. What was the probability of Twyla rolling a number below 5?

A. $\frac{2}{5}$ **B.** $\frac{1}{4}$ **C.** $\frac{2}{10}$ **D.** $\frac{5}{10}$

9. Imagine that all the dessert choices on the menu were written on separate pieces of paper, and these papers were put in a bag. You choose one dessert choice from the bag without looking. What would be the probability of choosing a dessert with chocolate?

A. $\frac{2}{8}$ **B.** $\frac{3}{8}$

C. $\frac{6}{10}$ **D.** $\frac{6}{15}$

10. Which tree diagram represents the dessert choices in Question 9?

A.

Type	Flavour
Cake	Chocolate / Apple / Blueberry
Ice cream	Vanilla / Chocolate
Pie	Lemon / Strawberry / Apple

B.

Type	Flavour
Cake	Blueberry / Chocolate / Raspberry
Ice cream	Vanilla / Chocolate / Blueberry
Pie	Strawberry / Lemon / Apple

C.

Type	Flavour
Cake	Chocolate / Raspberry
Ice cream	Vanilla / Chocolate
Pie	Strawberry / Lemon / Apple

D.

Type	Flavour
Cake	Blueberry / Chocolate / Raspberry
Ice cream	Vanilla / Chocolate
Pie	Strawberry / Lemon / Apple

Tiling an Area

Goal Tile an area using software.

1. How many congruent shapes will tile this area?
Use Geometer's Sketchpad or the grid below.

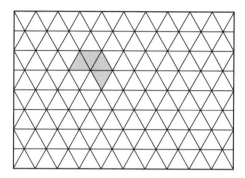

_____ congruent shapes

2. Tile the area below with this shape 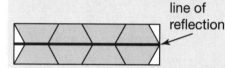 .

Cover as much of the area as possible. Use reflections only and show the lines of reflection on the grid.

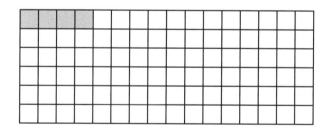

3. How would you move this shape ▢▢▢ to tile the lightly shaded area below?

Circle the correct answer.

translate 4 squares left

rotate 90° clockwise

translate 2 squares right and
1 square down

reflect about the horizontal

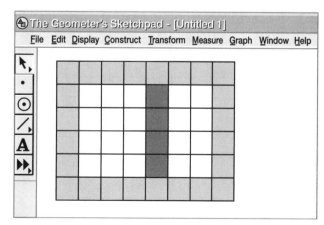

2 Describing Tiling Patterns

Goal Describe tiling patterns.

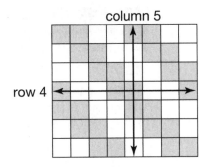

column 5

row 4

At-Home Help

A **tiling pattern** is a pattern of repeated congruent shapes that fit together with no gaps and no overlaps.

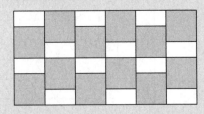

A **pattern rule** describes how you can reproduce a pattern.

For example, the pattern rule for the first column in the picture above is:

Start with 1 white rectangle, then 1 shaded square, 1 white rectangle, and 1 shaded square.

1. Which columns have different pattern rules? How do you know?

_____

_____

_____

_____

_____

2. Write a pattern rule for columns 5 and 7. How are the pattern rules the same? How are they different?

_____

_____

_____

_____

_____

3. Record the number of white and shaded tiles in each column. Use the table below.

Column	White tiles	Shaded tiles
1		
2		
3		
4		
5		
6		
7		
8		

3 Extending Tiling Patterns

Goal Write a pattern rule to extend a pattern.

1. Which pattern rule best describes the first row of this tiling pattern? Circle the correct answer.

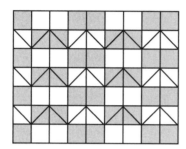

Start with 1 shaded tile, then alternate 1 white tile and 1 shaded tile.

Start with 1 white tile, then alternate 2 shaded tiles and 2 white tiles 4 times.

Start with 1 shaded tile, then alternate 2 white tiles and 2 shaded tiles 2 times.

Start with 1 white tile, then alternate 2 shaded tiles and 2 white tiles.

At-Home Help

A **pattern rule** states the starting point of a pattern, a description of the attributes that change, and the number of repetitions.

For example, the pattern rule for the first row is start with 1 shaded tile, then alternate 2 white tiles and 3 shaded tiles 3 times, and end with 2 white tiles.

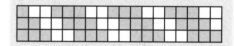

2. Look at the tiling pattern in Question 1. Write a pattern rule for any column.

_____

_____

3. Write a pattern rule for a row on this rug based on the letter F.

_____

_____

_____

_____

4 Translating Shapes on Grids

Goal Identify the rule for translating a shape.

1. Which statement best describes this translation? Circle the correct answer.

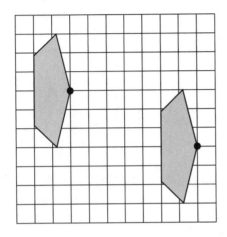

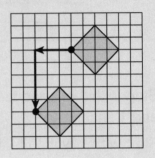
right 6 squares, down 3 squares

left 7 squares, up 4 squares

right 7 squares, down 3 squares

right 6 squares, down 2 squares

2. Greg wrote rules to describe the translation of a shape. Follow Greg's steps in the box.

   Show the result of each translation on the grid.

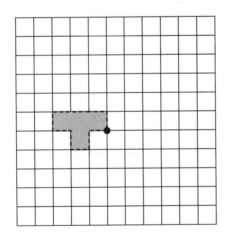

Start with a T-shape.

Step 1: right 6, down 2

Step 2: left 3, up 2

Step 3: left 3, down 2

Step 4: right 4, up 5

Step 5: up 2

Step 6: left 4

5 Rotating Shapes

Goal Rotate shapes in a pattern.

You will need a protractor and a ruler.

1. Which rotation rule was used? Circle the correct answer.

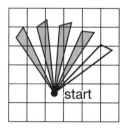

Rotate 20° counterclockwise 4 times.

Rotate 25° counterclockwise 4 times.

Rotate 20° counterclockwise 5 times.

Rotate 25° counterclockwise 5 times.

2. Chandra's Rotation Rule
Choose a vertex on the shape to be the centre of rotation. Rotate 25° counterclockwise 10 times.

Draw the logo using the rotation rule. Label the centre of rotation. Label the angle of rotation showing the direction.

3. A shape was rotated to create this logo.

a) Identify the centre of rotation. Label it on the logo.

b) What is the angle of rotation? Label it on the logo. _____

c) What is a possible direction of each rotation? Label it on the logo.

_____

Copyright © 2005 by Nelson Education Ltd.

At–Home Help

A **rotation** in 2-D is a turn about a point called the **centre of rotation**. When describing a rotation, remember to include both the angle and direction.

For example, this shape was rotated 90° counterclockwise.

90° counterclockwise

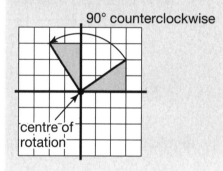

centre of rotation

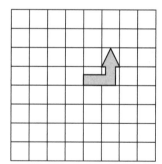

Communicate About Transformations

Goal Describe transformations using math language.

You will need a protractor and a ruler.

1. Name the transformation used to create shapes A, B, and C from the black shape.

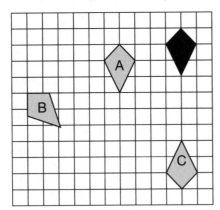

a) shape A _____

b) shape B _____

c) shape C _____

2. Look at the picture in Question 1. What kind of transformation is each student describing? Identify the shape by its letter. Explain how you know.

a) Isabelle: My transformation changed the orientation of the shape.

_____

_____

b) Zev: My transformation changed the position of every point on the shape.

_____

_____

_____

3. **a)** Copy the diagram on grid paper. Reflect it in the darker line.

   b) Describe the effect of the reflection.

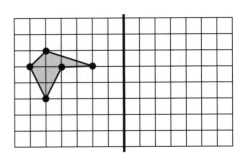

7 Modelling Congruence with Transformations

Goal **Show congruence using transformations.**

You will need a protractor and a ruler.

1. Circle the congruent shapes. Explain how you know. Use transformation language.

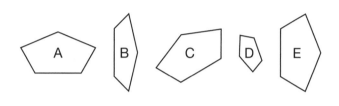

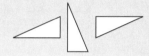
_____

_____

2.

a) Identify all sets of congruent shapes. Use the letters A, B, and C to show shapes that are congruent.

b) Describe the shape in each set.

_____

_____

_____

c) Choose one set of congruent shapes. Describe the transformations you used to show congruence.

_____

_____

_____

_____

_____

8 Exploring Similarity

Goal Identify similar figures using transformations.

You will need a ruler.

1. Two shapes were made using elastics. Why are these shapes similar?

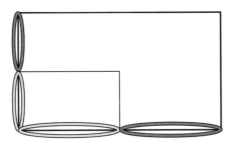

At-Home Help

Similar means the same shape but a different size.

For example, both trapezoids are similar.

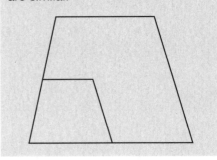

2. Yvette began to enlarge this triangle using elastics.

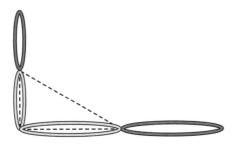

Draw the enlarged similar triangle.

3. What does a smaller similar triangle look like? Draw it.

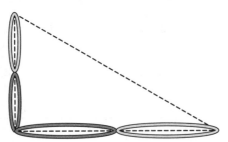

Test Yourself

Circle the correct answer.

1. How would you move this shape 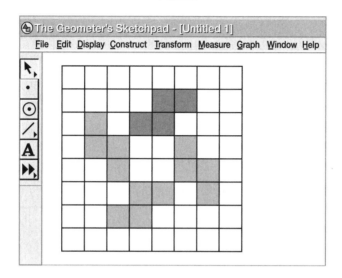 to tile the lightly shaded area below?

   A. translate down 3 squares and left 2 squares

   B. rotate 90° clockwise

   C. translate right 2 squares and down 3 squares

   D. reflect in a horizontal line

2. Which rows have a different pattern rule?

   A. rows 1 and 5

   B. rows 2 and 6

   C. rows 3 and 7

   D. rows 4 and 5

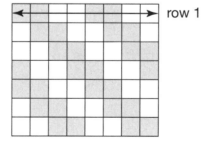

row 1

Test Yourself Page 2

3. Which statement best describes the translation shown?

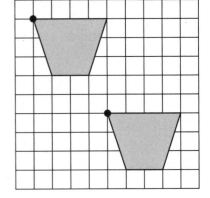

    A. translate right 6 squares and down 4 squares

    B. translate right 5 squares and down 4 squares

    C. translate left 5 squares and up 4 squares

    D. translate left 4 squares and up 5 squares

4. Which rotation rule was used to create the logo?

    A. Rotate 30° counterclockwise about B 5 times.

    B. Rotate 45° counterclockwise about O 7 times.

    C. Rotate 45° counterclockwise about A 5 times.

    D. Rotate 30° counterclockwise about O 7 times.

5. Which shapes are congruent and how do you know?

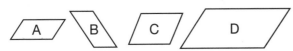

    A. Translate A to C and A covers C exactly.

    B. Rotate A to B and A covers B exactly.

    C. Reflect A to D and A covers D exactly.

    D. Translate A to B and A covers B exactly.

6. Look at the picture in Question 5. Which shapes are similar and how do you know?

    A. C is twice as large as B.

    B. C is twice as tall as A.

    C. D is twice as large as A.

    D. D is twice as tall as B.